# THE VOLKSKRANT BUILDING

## MANUFACTURING DIFFERENCE IN AMSTERDAM'S CREATIVE CITY

Boukje Cnossen & Sebastian Olma

# COLOPHON

· · · · · · · · · · · · · · · · · · · · · · · · · · · · · · · · · · · · · · · · · · · · · · · · · · · · · · · · · · · · · ·

**Boukje Cnossen and Sebastian Olma**
**The Volkskrant Building: Manufacturing Difference in Amsterdam's Creative City**

**Production** Miriam Rasch
**Design** UNDOG, Amsterdam
**EPUB development** André Castro
**Copy-editor** Margarita Osipian
**Printer** Offsetdrukkerij Nuance
**Publisher** Amsterdam Creative Industries Publishing, Rose Leighton
**Supported by** Amsterdam University of Applied Sciences (Hogeschool van Amsterdam), Stichting Urban Resort, University of Amsterdam, Bureau Broedplaatsen (Municipality of Amsterdam), Institute of Network Cultures.
**Cover image** A door of one of the studios in the art factory. Picture by Tanja Sihvonen.
**Photography** Bambos Demetriou (*p. 42*), Louk Heimans (*p. 74*), Raymond van Mil (*p. 54*), Tanja Sihvonen (*p. 6, 8, 64, 76*), Unknown (*p. 14, 16, 28*)

**Contact** Amsterdam Creative Industries Publishing, www.amsterdamcreativeindustries.com

EPUB and PDF editions of this publication are freely downloadable from our website.



Amsterdam, November 2014

**ISBN** 978-94-92171-00-9 (print)
**ISBN** 978-94-92171-01-6 (epub)

# CONTENTS


Introduction: A Story of Transformation ............................................................. 9
Origins: Spring 2007 and Before ...................................................................... 17
Cash-Stripped Bohemia: 2007-2009 ............................................................... 29
Networks of Creative Production: 2009-2013 ................................................ 43
Enter the Volkshotel: 2013 and Onwards ........................................................ 55
Conclusion: Failing Forward ............................................................................ 65

Announcement warning against theft in one of the hallways of the buildings.

## ACKNOWLEDGEMENTS

First and foremost we would like to thank Urban Resort for their support in realizing this book. It was a great joy working with them. Our special thanks go to the people of the Volkskrant building; all the tenants but also those running Canvas and the Volkshotel. Without their willingness to participate in our research, this book would have been impossible. Bureau Broedplaatsen has kindly contributed to the publication process and we are very grateful for this. We would also like to thank the Faculty of the Humanities at the University of Amsterdam, in particular CIRCA, for financing and facilitating the majority of the research for this book. For the production and publication of the book we are greatly indebted to the Amsterdam University of Applied Sciences, in particular to Miriam Rasch of the Institute of Network Cultures whose professional support, enthusiasm and encouragement were absolutely vital for making this book happen. Thanks to Margarita Osipian for proofing the text and to the Industries Publishing division of the Amsterdam Creative Industries Network for their brilliant support and speed in turning our manuscript into a publication.

The entrance to the fifth floor of the art factory in the former Volkskrant building, built and painted by the tenants of this floor.

# INTRODUCTION: A STORY OF TRANSFORMATION

This book tells the story of the Volkskrant building and how it became an 'art factory'. 'Art factory' is a slightly inspired translation of the Dutch term *broedplaats* (literally: breeding place). It refers to a subsidized space for creative production. In the case of the Volkskrant building, however, the term art factory pretty much nailed it. In the six years of its existence, the building hosted many, by now well-known, manufacturers of art, such as the world-travelling DJ Tom Trago, the internationally exhibited artist Wayne Horse, and the successful hip hop label Killing Skills. It was also a place where some of Amsterdam's greatest art and music festivals were produced, such as the Burning Man-inspired Magneetfestival, performance festival De Parade, the Klik Animation Festival, and hip hop festival Appelsap. But most importantly, it was the place to be in Amsterdam for anyone who wanted to tune into the beat of art and subculture.

As with all publicly subsidized art factories, the Volkskrant Building was always meant to be a temporary creative space. In 2012, after 5 years of being an art factory, the building was sold to an entrepreneur and property investor who have used the creative image of the place in order to turn it into a cultural hotel. Although this illustrates the use that the arts have for commercial endeavors, the story of the art factory does not end here. The name of the hotel - Volkshotel - reminds of the buildings former function and a smaller art factory will continue to be part of the building and is effectively subsidized by the hotel business. With this rather unique business model, the aim is to keep the creative weirdness of the art factory. Whether this is indeed going to happen is not a question we can answer. However, we believe this development to be remarkable enough to document the processes that changed this building from a practically worthless office structure into a creative hotspot of serious interest to big property developers. The analysis of these processes and their effects are the subject of this book.

The Volkskrant building, perhaps more than any other place throughout the city, exemplifies Amsterdam's transformation into a 'creative city' over the past fifteen years. During the course of its recent career - from a newspaper office to an art factory, and finally to an arty hotel - the building was a nexus of the dreams, struggles and realities involved in Amsterdam's emergence as one of Europe's most paradigmatic creative cities. This, as many an observer has remarked, has less to do with the city adopting those policies than it has with the city's history as a fiercely liberal and freethinking town.[1] Amsterdam's magnetic pull to the rest of the world has always had a lot to do with it being a place for radicals, outcasts and indeed, creatives. This started in the 17th century, when Amsterdam was the economic center of the world, and resurfaced in a completely different way in 1967 during what became known as the Summer of Love. Some places are still trying to maintain some of the city's characteristic craziness. The Volkskrant building was - and hopefully will continue to be - one of them.

* * * * * * * *

The building was a nexus of the dreams, struggles and realities
involved in Amsterdam's emergence as one of Europe's most
paradigmatic creative cities.

* * * * * * * *

We provide a look behind the façade of the Volkskrant building, an honest account of the conflicts and struggles, the parties and projects, the transformation of dreams into reality. This account is intended as a document of critical contemporary history and offers insights into the workings of the creative economy.

**The Volkskrant Building and the Creative City**

The transformation of the former newspaper office into an art factory began in 2007. At this moment, the idea of the 'creative city' was starting to become influential as a policy approach all over Europe. The creative city paradigm emerged from the intersection of two different developments. One was the political creation of the creative industries as a new economic sector. Originally an initiative of Tony Blair's New Labour government, creative industries policies quickly started to spread throughout the European continent. The goal of these policies was to unify all those economic activities connected to the generation and exploitation of intellectual property where, it was argued, the future of economic growth was to be found and the prosperity of cities ensured.[2] The other development had to do with the idea of using artists and creatives more actively within the processes of urban planning and development. Popularized by academics like Richard Florida, the 'creative class' became a crucial reference among city officials, denoting a new breed of entrepreneurs and professionals which cities needed to attract in order to remain competitive.[3] In the imagination of policy makers, artistic professionals and creative entrepreneurs could become an engine of economic transformation and urban regeneration. Yet, for this to happen, a new urban infrastructure was required that catered to the needs of these creative producers.

In this context, the Volkskrant building's art factory seemed to provide a perfect example of creative city transformation. As a 'best-practice' case, it was featured in presentations and publications of policy experts, consultants, and academics in order to illustrate the successful combination of artistic and entrepreneurial creativity. Just as it happened with similar creative development projects, in the Netherlands as well as internationally, the Volkskrant building was often reduced to a couple of PowerPoint slides and a corresponding list of 'success factors'. While such references are usually well-meaning, they remain superficial. In fact, it is quite disturbing to see how little professional interest there has been in the actual practices that go on behind the funky façades of the creative city. We wonder: if one wants to design policies catering to the needs of creative labor and entrepreneurship, what could be more pressing than doing research into the everyday realities of creative production?

If it is true, as the pundits do not tire to tell us, that we are in the middle of massive social, economic, and cultural transformations, then surely no one expects policy makers, pioneers, and first-movers to get everything right the first time around. What we do expect, though, is a rigorous analysis of policies and practices for the sake of their improvement. Such rigorous analysis should start from a careful observation of the day-to-day creative, strategic, and material practices that, together, make up the creative industries, as they have become known. Success or failure of the creative transformation of our cities and economies depends for a large part on learning from one's mistakes. Right now, we do not see this happening enough.

Not being naïve, we do understand that there are a variety of reasons for this omission. Critical research into economic practice has always been a difficult endeavor, given the business interests at stake. The idea of inter-city competition, which is at the heart of the creative city paradigm, does not help to spread a critical ethos among public institutions either. Always wary of one's market value vis-à-vis supposedly competing cities, officials prefer to work with docile consultants and professional researchers who deliver a positive outlook. At the same time, universities have a hard time adjusting their programs to the interdisciplinary challenges that come with the new topologies of creative labor and entrepreneurship. Increasingly commercialized funding structures do not help this situation either. As a result, we see a lot of infrastructural change in our cities but we are not able to properly assess it.

With this book we would like to contribute to a much needed debate around the creative city. Although we are aware that ours is a modest effort, we hope to help deliver some empirical substance to an emerging critical discussion. This discussion was articulated recently, for instance, in an intervention by Roel Griffioen[4], where the author argues that many of the art factories placed in less vibrant areas are essentially vehicles for a neoliberal version of social work, in which the presence of artists and their projects must act as a cheaper form of community work. Without denying or confirming this thesis, we open the black box of the art factory in order to take a better look at the very practices allegedly making up this neoliberal creative city. We also believe that the case of the Volkskrant building has a significance that goes beyond questions of the making of the creative city. Because the Volkskrant building was about more than the generation of artistic and economic value, it provided an infrastructure for experimentation with more active and participatory forms of citizenship. We argue that, in order to understand the full implication of the art factory, we must not overlook the political dimension of those things happening within the building.

**The City from Below**

When politicians and policy makers talk about the importance of creative spaces, they usually talk about things like entrepreneurship, technology or city marketing. Whatever they refer to, their vision of the creative city is always clean and sane. Artists and creatives are portrayed as happy participants in their city's economy, spending their days canvassing business models, and feeding the market the latest tech-experiences. But what they tend to forget is that the most radical innovations do not come out of shiny offices but are forged on the strange fringes of mainstream culture. This limited vision of creativity is an omission in many European cities, but in Amsterdam it is an insult to the city's history. It is no exaggeration to say that the contemporary art and culture scenes owe a substantial part of their existence to the past and - now illegal - present squatter scenes and their adjacent networks.

. . . . . . . .

The most radical innovations do not come out of shiny offices but
are forged on the strange fringes of mainstream culture.

. . . . . . . .

Someone who understood this very well was the American geographer Edward Soja, who visited Amsterdam in 1990. During his stay in the Dutch capital, he carefully observed the squats on the Spuistraat, where he was living at the time. In the essay that resulted from these observations, he states that the squatters movement was more than just an occupation of abandoned offices, factories, warehouses, and some residencies. 'It was a fight for the rights to the city itself, especially for the young and for the poor. Nowhere has this struggle been more successful than in Amsterdam'.[5] Looking at the narrow stairwells and compact spaces of the houses so typical of Amsterdam's city center, Soja noted that 'the patient preservation yet modernization of these monuments reflects that "original genius" of the Dutch to make big things of little spaces, to literally produce an enriching and communal urban spatiality through aggressive social intervention and grass-roots planning, an adaptive feat on par with the Dutch conquest of the sea'.[6] For Soja, the squatted communities that, in 1990, were all over the Amsterdam city, were indicative of a phenomenon particular to Amsterdam. In order to better understand this, Soja picked up on the British historian Simon Schama's notion of 'moral geography', characterized as 'an uncanny skill in working against the prevailing tides and times to create places that reinforce collective self-recognition and identity'.[7] His main argument was that, in the case of Amsterdam, the groups that could be called countercultural or underground have in fact always collaborated with the existing powers in order to create these places of self-recognition.

What Soja observed in the early 90s was the result of a long tradition of alternative movements through which a practice of radical, yet pragmatic, appropriation of space was established in the post-war period. As we will see in the first chapter of this book, this is the culture out of which the Volkskrant building emerged and this is also the culture that forms the foundation of Amsterdam as a creative city.

**Creative Catch 22**

The Volkskrant building was realized by a handful of ex-squatters who, over the course of the project and with the support of the city, turned into real estate developers. These squatters cum property developers infused this space with the dose of weirdness and mild insanity that - as we have said above - has always been one of the reasons for Amsterdam's attractiveness as a city. Taking on the name Urban Resort, the ex-squatters built an organization that was able to carry some of the old Amsterdam craziness into the future.

Since 2000, the Amsterdam city government has featured a department that goes by the name *Bureau Broedplaatsen* [the Art Factory Bureau]. It has been responsible for exploring the potential of vacant property for the creative sector, as well as funding and facilitating the re-development of appropriate buildings. Today, the Art Factory Bureau has contributed to the realization of more than 3500 individual creative work spaces divided over more than fifty locations throughout the city. Urban Resort, the main character of this book, has had an ambiguous relationship with the Art Factory Bureau. On the one hand, they wanted to participate in the mainstream creative economy in order to show everyone that they, quite literally, mean business. On the other hand, they wanted to provide an alternative to that. This book explores this tension in further detail.

Urban Resort has had an ambiguous relationship
with the Art Factory Bureau.

The physical takeover of space, appropriating and shaping it according to one's own wishes, is something that Urban Resort had stimulated their tenants to do from the very beginning. Coming from a squatting background, one of their principles when setting up the art factory in the Volkskrant building was self-management. Squatted communities or other autonomous social spaces were, and still are, often run on the basis of self-management. This means that democratic processes steer who is responsible for what, which ultimately puts the collective at the top of the organizational structure. And by running a space together, new social ties can be formed. As one of the founders puts it: 'You have to allow people to adapt their space. If you paint a hallway together, you will start to talk about other things than work'. In the case of the Volkskrant building, Urban Resort's emphasis on self-management also had very practical reasons. As people would clean and take care of maintenance issues as a collective, rent could be kept low. However, as we will see over the course of

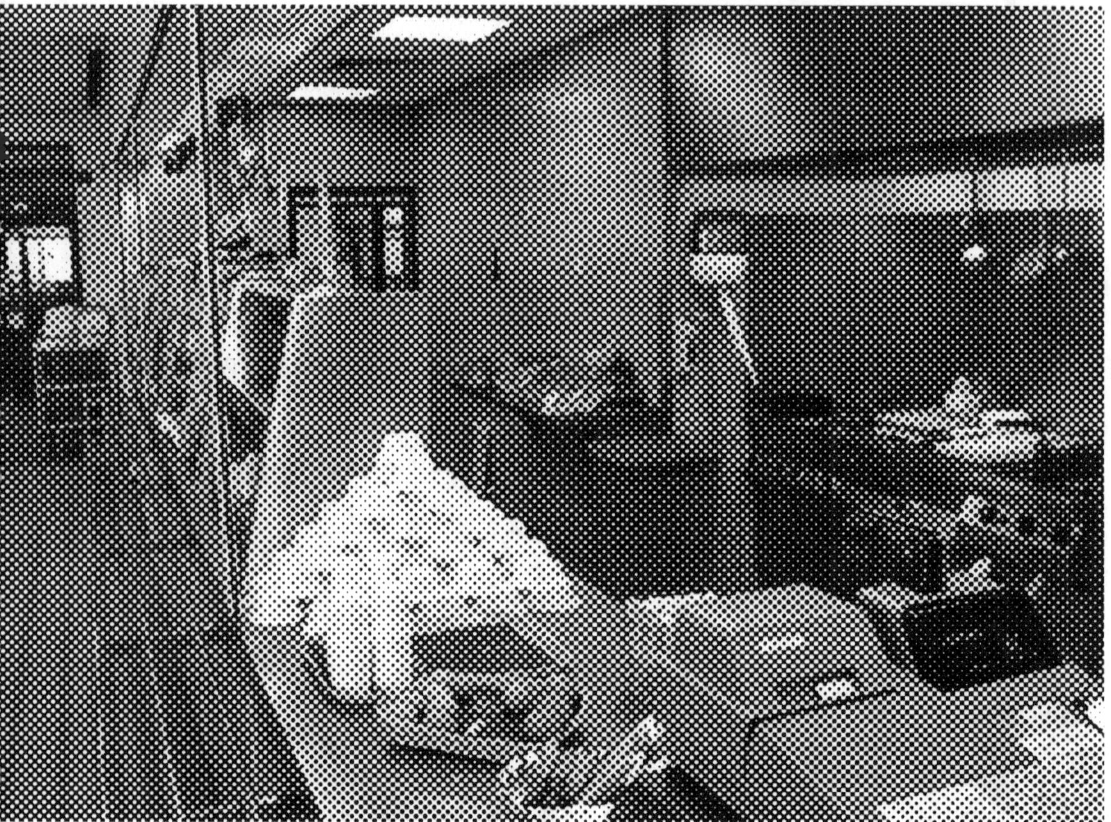

The staff restaurant on the top floor as photographed during one of Urban Resort's exploratory visits to the building in 2007.

the book, many of these initial ideas had to be altered according to the demands of today's creative professionals.

Setting up creative spaces, formerly done by squatters, has now become serious business for more mainstream property developers as well. This begs the question: if it does not happen at the borders of legality, but rather out in the open, with commercial interests and instigated with public money, does it work? And if so, how? Before we delve into the detailed descriptions of the events of the Volkskrant building and the historical background of stakeholders involved, we want to emphasize the fact that the practices that came to shape the art factory often contradicted the policies allowing their existence. These often unresolved and perhaps unresolvable tensions formed a sort of political background for the day-to-day operations of the art factory. Even if they went unnoticed by many of the tenants, they determined, to a large extent, the course of life of the Volkskrant building. We will return to this question in our concluding chapter, where we turn to a more theoretical reflection on our research material regarding the relation between urban infrastructure and citizenship, drawing on the work of Richard Sennett, Peter Sloterdijk and Paolo Virno.

Most of the research for this book took place between July 2012 and May 2013. The material we used consists of field notes from intensive participant observation on a four-day-per-week basis, more than sixty semi-structured interviews with tenants, extensive interviews with the staff and management of Urban Resort, and several focus groups. This was supplemented with archival material, as well as material from conversations with policy-makers, property developers, relevant cultural entrepreneurs, and other stakeholders who have provided the context in which the building's communities took shape.

Doing research during the transitional period in which the building went from being a subsidized art factory to becoming a commercial art-flavored hotel has helped us understand the dynamics between those to whom the building is an investment, those to whom it is a political tool, and those who 'simply' go there to work. It has led us to conclude that, although the differences in interest are evident and relevant, the common denominator between these parties is that eventually, they all wanted the place to be interesting. And as we will see over the course of this book, it is precisely in deciphering the meaning of the adjective 'interesting' that we find clues about the value of places like the Volkskrant building.

One of the remaining squats in the Spuistraat, situated in the city center of Amsterdam.

**Chapter 1**

# ORIGINS: SPRING 2007 AND BEFORE

The story of the Volkskrant building, as we will tell it, started in March 2007. One afternoon, a small group of squatters gathered in front of an office building east of Amsterdam's city center on the windy and traffic-packed Wibautstraat. Saying that they were out of practice would be an understatement. Although some of them still lived in squats, the times of breaking into buildings and occupying them were long gone. However, they still cared about the vitality of the city. Otherwise why would they be here, considering to 'do something', no one knew exactly what, with the boring office building in front of them? Among them was Jaap Draaisma, who remembered the feeling of the squatting days; that they were changing not just their city, but the entire world along with it. 'It was crisis everywhere. In some countries, for instance Chile and Portugal, communist systems were installed democratically. It was possible to think that revolution was really about to happen'.

Now the talk of revolution had ceased for good. The tables had turned and now the city government informed the squatters that this building was empty. How the former opponents ended up working together so closely is an interesting story. What's more is that it plays a big role in what the Volkskrant building would later become: an odd mixture of urban counterculture, the government's successful attempt at taming it, and property investors eventually benefiting from the results. But before it gets to that point, we should understand how rebellious squatters started to rub shoulders with officials long before that moment in March 2007 on the Wibautstraat.

**Places of Collective Self-Recognition**
In his essay observing the legalized squats on the Spuistraat in Amsterdam, the American geographer Edward Soja argued that, in Amsterdam, countercultural groups had always collaborated with the existing powers in order to create and maintain their 'places of self-recognition'.[8] Vice versa, the city government at a certain point had started to notice the value of the movements that challenged them, and decided to organize those disruptive powers in order to mobilize them for the sake of the entire city. Soja's observation will be helpful to the reader

who is not familiar with the complex dialectic, that is particular to Amsterdam, between the former squatters and the city government. It is against this backdrop that the development of the Volkskrant building has to be understood. Let's take yet another look at those former squatters as they are standing in front of the Volkskrant building in the afternoon of March 2007. Hein de Haan for instance, had become an associate professor in urban planning. Hay Schoolmeesters had worked as a cultural organizer on the NDSM-wharf, one of the city's formerly industrial wharfs, and Eric Duivenvoorden had published various books on the history of the squatters movement.[9] Jaap Draaisma had worked as a civil servant for one of the city's boroughs. But while all of them are holding so-called 'decent jobs', each of them nonetheless continued to fight for the legalization and protection of squatted places. Only they had resorted to more legal, and less tiresome, ways.







So would they be up for converting such a big building into a creative community? Time, it seems, was on their side. Amsterdam's officials were finally listening to them. Since the nineties, the economy was booming and Amsterdam chose to redevelop its waterfront into a prestigious skyline. This meant getting rid of the remaining squats that had settled in the old warehouses around the harbor. The tight network that remained from the squatters movement, and of which our protagonists are a part, protested against this, but to no avail. Now, as a way of making it up to them, the city government was giving them a chance to show what they were capable of.

**'Breeding Places'**
The city has asked them to set up a so-called *broedplaats*, a term idiosyncratic to the Amsterdam context at that time. A *broedplaats* is something in between an incubator and an artistic residency. It literally translates as 'breeding place' but the Amsterdam city government uses the term 'art factory' in their English documents. This policy, so the squatters were thinking, would enable them not only to set up an autonomous community without the risk of being evicted, but it would give them funding from the city on top of that.

So as they found themselves contemplating the rather boring looking building that would soon become empty, their hands were definitely itching. It was a chance to prove what they were capable of. To contribute to the city's diversity by making room for artistic experiments, cultural exchanges, and countercultural manifestations. A space devoid of the dominant economic rationale, where social and cultural values would be more important than financial gain. If only they had known what they signed up for.

Hay Schoolmeesters had his doubts. Being the rookie of the gang, Hay recalls planning for a year-long sabbatical when Draaisma asked him to join him in setting up the Volkskrant building. 'I looked up at the Volkskrant building. The newspaper *De Volkskrant* still had to move out, so we could only see it from the outside. I remember thinking: it is too big, too ugly and too... office-like. We had experience with warehouses, enormous empty halls where you simply draw lines on the floor in order to determine who gets what space. No lifts, no complicated heating or ventilation system, and especially no carpets and no having to make a fuss about half a square meter', says Hay.

The others agreed that the building was far from ideal, but had good reasons to be tempted. 'The aim was to use this building in order to prove to Amsterdam that it was still possible to establish interesting social and cultural communities based on a lot of freedom and with a solid exposure to the neighborhood and the city.



The Volkskrant building would serve as a starting point. From there we would extend our practice all over the city', Hay recalls. Although this is, in a way, what happened, none of them could foresee how difficult it would become. Over the course of the next chapters we will learn all about it. Suffice to say for now that, although these six squatters lack the legal and managerial skill needed to run a place that is not a squat, their desire to make it happen is unstoppable. In a sense, they still look at the city the way squatters do: as a battle field.

**The Battle for the City**
As in many other cities, the Amsterdam squatters movement emerged in the 70s out of the need for affordable housing. Although political and ideological motivation would soon start to play a big role, squatting did not start off as a political movement per se. The book *Beweg-ingsleer* [Kinematics] is a rich and strange document of this time, trying to provide a real-time account of the events as they unravelled. The anonymous authors go to great length explaining that the squatters movement was not a singular, well-defined movement, but instead con-sisted of the convergence of several scenes, which were concerned with different causes and directed different types of energy towards these causes.

> Everyone defines the beginning and the end of "the squatters movement" differently. This is because everyone entered the common space in a different place. For some this happened by breaking the door into their own flat, for others it happened while drifting through the in-finite voids of the urban complexes that were squatted with a large group. Every squatter can indicate the place where she or he crossed the threshold and entered a collective space.[10]

Even though the initial motivations among squatters might have been diffuse, it was through the practice of occupying space that a common purpose emerged. The experience of being able to appropriate a little piece of the city as an exercise in communal activism seemed to open a window of some sort of opportunity into the future. In the words of the authors of *Bewegingsleer*: 'In the midst of the city, among the concrete shapes of everyday ennui, one could enter a space of unlimited possibilities'.[11]

This shift from an almost accidental entrance into the movement, to the realization that squatting enables you to do things differently, was certainly what happened to Jaap Draaisma. He initially became a squatter simply because he needed a place to live. After spending only a week in a squatted building that was then evicted, Jaap ended up in another squat and realized the political nature of the movement. Jaap: 'They were real hippies. They created meditation rooms in all these squats, with incense and what have you. There was a lot of escapism to it, with their drugs and communes. I grew up in an area that was rather poor and sympathetic to the communists because of all the social work they did. Communists did not want to escape, they wanted to take over. Coming from that background, I thought these hippies were rather decadent'. The hippies Jaap refers to were Amsterdam's so-called Kabouters, who had emerged out of the Provo movement. At the end of the 1970s, their manifestations, and the atmosphere of freedom and possibility that came with it, attracted young people from all over the world to the city. Perhaps in a peculiar way they could be seen as the alternative and anti-commercial precursors of the later prophets of the gospel of the creative class.[12]

Despite his ideological fervor, the way Jaap finally became one of the central figures of the squatters movement was quite pedestrian. It started in 1975 when he was renting a room, legally, in the city center, and received the message that he and his housemates had to vacate. Jaap: 'Squatting was becoming more and more common at that point, and we decided we could be tough too. So we put up a banner on the outside of the property saying "We Are Staying". All of a sudden, we had become squatters. I started to negotiate on behalf of our group with the landlord, and it turned out the city government owned the building. I dealt with the press, got a grasp of how local politics work. I learned a great deal from that'.

Squatting exploded at the end of the 1970s. 'The movement went from hundreds to thousands of people' Jaap recalls. They quickly built up their own universe within the city, as we learn again from *Bewegingsleer*:

· · · · · · · · ·

'The movement went from hundreds to thousands of people'.

· · · · · · · · ·

Within the realm of squatting there was no sense of historical development, only the realization that one could find the same thing in an increasing number of places, including the weirdest corners of the city. Once you had entered you would be surprised to find so many more people in the same spot, as crazy, radical, and amateur as you were, surprised to see the cool pragmatism with which the most heated desire for action was executed. The space could literally be found in and outside of "the governing system". "The city was ours", because it was embedded within our own topology of secret signposts: buildings, cafes, haberdashers, vendors, cycling routes, streets and bridges, symbols, signals, posters, traditional clothing and hairstyles. The smell of damp leather jackets and shower-less houses, cat urine, plastic bags with car mirrors, stolen traffic signs [...]. A spider web of backyards, staircases, coffee and booze drinking sessions, joints and trips, stencils, stolen books, press lists, breaking into TV stations, helmets and bats, breaking tiles, vans and carrier cycles [...].[13]

The way this odd assemblage functioned was through so-called squatting groups. Each of them was in charge of an area of the city and prepared actions for that area, such as those during the coronation of the Dutch Queen Beatrix in 1980. 'In the month before we had squatted 120 houses in Amsterdam', Jaap recalls. Invoking violent encounters with the police, this day showed that the city had truly become a battleground.

But the battle was about more than space. Jaap: 'At the beginning of the 80s, the establishment was completely stuck. We were convinced that we would take over the power. We did not know how, but we were absolutely certain that it would happen. And there was proof that the world as we knew it was collapsing. Amsterdam was practically a third world city. Back then, at the beginning of the 1980s, nobody wanted to invest a penny in the city'.

### 'Grutters' and Alternative Economies

Although squats represented a different vision of reality, it was still not clear what that reality was supposed to look like. This changed when some of the squats started to play a serious role in the city's cultural life. Today, concert venues Melkweg and Paradiso, which were squatted in the 1970s, are still bearing testimony to the cultural contributions that have come from the squatters movement. Another major cultural venue at the time was Wijers, which existed between 1981 and 1984.[14] The biggest squat ever running in the Netherlands was located close to Amsterdam's central railway station. It housed around a hundred small companies, from galleries and studios to a concert hall fitting twelve hundred people.

The experience of a place in which things were happening led the squatters to believe they could create new economies. As such, squats could benefit not just the people living there but the wider city too. 'At Wijers, an alternative economy was emerging', Jaap, who had started to organize concerts there, recalled. 'Around 200 people were able to make a living from being part of our community. We were almost self-sufficient. The chamber of commerce and local politicians took interest in what we were doing. The economy we were creating had to be one on our terms: with money, but without interest. With property, but always collectively owned. We were following euro-communist thinkers such as the current Italian president Napolitano, who believed that the world could be taken over through gradual immersion into all institutions, rather than through a violent revolution'.

The conviction that it was not just about squatting, but about setting up culturally interesting communities, became the ideological basis for the many legalizations of squats between 1981 and 1984. Many of these were initiated by squatters themselves, Jaap being one of them. 'We made smart use of new policies aimed at creating social housing for young people. This way we managed to legalize and renovate hundreds of squats, so that the squatters who lived there became legal tenants', he says.



The obvious advantage of legalization was that the alternative communities were no longer threatened in their existence. But some of the more radical strands within the squatters movement were against the idea of business altogether, and therefore did not want to become business owners themselves. Conflict and division arose within the movement and in the more radical quarters. Jaap was seen as a sell-out. 'All those squats wanted their own cafe, a stage, and an exhibition space, but the radicals were against this because it meant you had to deal with licenses and regulations. If you complied with those things, you risked being taken for a petty shopkeeper, or a "grutter", as the Dutch slang of the time said'.[15]

Wijers would become a sort of blueprint for the Volkskrant building. Alderman Maarten van Poelgeest, in charge of urban planning in Amsterdam between 2006 and 2014, already recognized the value the place had for the city at the time. In an interview with Dutch daily newspaper *De Volkskrant* he mentions Wijers as an inspiration for his later support of art factories: 'I had just come to Amsterdam to study. Wijers represented the constructive part of the squatters movement, which created new meanings for old property and did something worthwhile for the city. It is a shame Wijers did not make it'.[16] In a way, the experience Van Poelgeest had visiting Wijers as a student led to him supporting art factories in his political career.

While Wijers was proof that the squatters movement was not just about protest but also about creation, its success was very much shaped by the lack of opportunities the regular economy offered at the time. It provided an infrastructure where people experienced an alternative culture and economy that also gave them the opportunity for individual and collective experimentation within changing societal conditions. 'We gradually had to let go of the idea of revolution, simply because capitalism started to gain territory again. People wanted to live in the city again, the market got back on its feet. By the end of the 80s I had to conclude society wasn't as hermetic as I had thought and that we could find spaces of opportunity within that system. It took some years to get to that conclusion', Jaap says. Over the course of this book, it will become clear that the trajectory of the Volkskrant building cannot simply be understood in terms of a relationship between two static forces, the alternative scene on one side, and the mainstream on the other, but that these two sides (to use simplified terms) continuously shape each other as well. The alternative scene constantly had to reinvent itself according to current political and economic circumstances.

## From Attacking 'The System' to Protecting Subculture

To summarize, the Amsterdam squatters movement first fought for their own places of self-recognition, to return to Soja's phrasing. Via the 'grutter'-approach of setting up small alternative businesses and cultural venues, they ended up living in a paradox of places that claimed to be autonomous, yet needed the city's toleration to be sustained.

Instead of taking over the system, as they once intended, the squatters had carved out their own zones within that system. Those places not only provided inexpensive living space, but also helped towards diversifying urban cultural life. Everything seemed to be smooth sailing. But it never hurts to look to one's laurels. During the 1990s, as the property market was reaching a peak, it was decided that almost all alternative cultural venues around the harbor that had come out of the squatting scene and had settled into warehouses, such as the Graansilo and Pakhuis Amerika, had to disappear. A group of local politicians and officials had been inspired by a field trip to cities such as Baltimore and Boston in the United States,[17] and felt that the shores of the IJ, as the harbor's water is called, had to become the city's eye-catcher. The alderman responsible for this was Duco Stadig, a Dutch Labor Party politician who was in charge of urban planning between 1994 and 2006. Jaap Draaisma remembers not being amused with Stadig's plans: 'According to him, all squats had to go. He did not see any added value in them at all'. Duco Stadig himself has a more nuanced memory of that time. 'Some buildings could stay, others were demolished. We actually renovated Pakhuis de Zwijger, which was squatted, with an enormous amount of money. This would never have been possible now'.

· · · · · · · ·

They ended up living in a paradox of places that claimed to be
autonomous, yet needed the city's toleration to be sustained.

· · · · · · · ·

The issue of the waterfront warehouses brought a more widespread discontent with the ongoing gentrification of Amsterdam to the surface. Duco Stadig felt he had to do something with that. 'The city made a lot of money by selling land for office locations, not just on the IJ-shore, because companies were willing to pay a lot for that at the time'. In 1999, he convinced the city council to put 90 million guilders (45 million euros) aside. This budget would become the basis of the art factory policy. This certainly started as a strategic move, because, in Duco's own words: 'Putting aside a lot of money gave me a good position in the public debate. Although the squats at the IJ had to go, I could say that we offered an alternative'.

But the former alderman was also convinced that what happens at the fringes of a city can be of importance. Duco Stadig:

In 1995 I visited an exhibition in a squat. I entered a very large room full of enormous art works. The person who was giving me the tour said that that was the studio of Peter Klashorst [a successful Dutch visual artist], who was about to leave because he was having his breakthrough. This is when I realized: it is really about those few instances that someone reaches the top from a broad foundation. You don't know who that will be, so you must nurture that entire foundation.

So the money was abundant and there was no lack of Florida-like good intentions either. But the real discussion, about what to do with all this money, still had to start. The city council founded a feedback group with the title Project Group Art Factory, comprising of several members from the squatters movement, among which were Urban Resort-founders Hein de Haan and Hessel Dokkum. Throughout 2000, their meetings took place at ADM, arguably the most outstanding squat in Amsterdam and accidentally the place where another Urban Resort founder, Hay Schoolmeesters, also lives until this day. Jaap Schoufour, who would later become head of the Art Factory Bureau, recalls the odd mixture of people. 'There were two types of people in that group, really. Some said you should never talk to the city government, because it is against the essence of squatting. Others, for example the eventual initiators of Urban Resort, wanted to be practical and discuss things with us'.

· · · · · · · ·

'No Culture Without Subculture'

· · · · · · · ·

Out of this group emerged a plan with the title 'No Culture Without Subculture'. It was presented to the city council on June 21, 2000 and would become the basis of the art factory policy.[18] The document was full of pictures of artworks placed outdoors, artisans and craftsmen working on tribal-looking objects, and communal areas of squat-like places. The text also showed that the ideas for the policy were coming straight out of the experience people had had in the (legalized) squats:

These places have a role as the incubators of creativity for artists, craftsmen and cultural entrepreneurs. These places also supplement the facilities in the neighborhood (for instance by providing a dining facility, a community theatre, etc.). They are often characterized by large, tall spaces, with a low rent which offers an opportunity to those groups that cannot afford a workspace in the regular market. Such places serve a purpose for the city, for instance by strengthening the social infrastructure. These (living and) workspaces enlarge the quality, diversity and image of an area, they "produce" culture, which adds to the cultural richness of the city, they facilitate synergy between different cultural entrepreneurs and their environment, which will be strengthened even more if people live in these buildings as well, and the social climate of the area is improved by offering these facilities to the neighborhood.[19]

The overall tone of the document is one of entitlement. If the city government had taken away the underground cultural venues and was now offering a consolation prize in return, then surely the people from those evicted places should be first in line to receive it. It therefore caused quite the shock when the newly installed art factory policy and accompanying funds were not used to prevent the disappearance of the already existing places that met the requirements of the new policy.

## The Battle Continues

Although beautiful plans and generous budgets were bringing officials and squatters closer together, this was not the end of painful conflicts between the city and the squatters scene. In fact, the most violent encounter between police and squatters in a very long time was about to take place. In October 2000, twelve adjacent squats known as the Calendar Buildings were being evicted for the sake of expensive new developments. This large complex full of artistic activity was situated on a popular spot in the city center, just in front of Amsterdam's zoo. So although the city had just promised to protect and fund alternative cultural venues, the project developer had other plans.

. . . . . . . . .

*This was not the end of painful conflicts between the city and the squatters scene.*

. . . . . . . . .

Bas van de Geyn, who would later manage the Volkskrant building for Urban Resort, was an active member of the community hosted by the Calendar Buildings. Previously he had been involved in Berlin's famous Wohnzimmerbar movement in the late 90s:

> In Berlin, we would choose an area that had almost nothing going on and set up bars in living rooms. It is the type of thing that everyone knows Berlin for now, but at the time it was novel. We would just put on some music, have some discussions and people came. When I returned to Amsterdam, I thought the city was in desperate need of something similar. So I started to organize artistic evenings in the Calendar Buildings. We charged a small entrance fee and programmed between thirty and forty acts in one night, from punk bands to fine art exhibits, to independent documentaries. We were very ambitious.

It was at the Calendar Buildings that he met Jaap Draaisma, who was running a martial arts center there. Jaap says the place reminded him of Wijers. 'There were concerts, an entire alternative economy could be found there'. When it became apparent the new owner had a plan for the large complex, Jaap ran into Duco Stadig again. Duco assured him there was no other option than to evict the buildings. 'It was not as if we did not want to do anything for the creative underclass, to phrase it that way, but we simply could not do anything there because the buildings had been squatted after the redevelopment project had been signed for', says Duco.

While Jaap tried to convince the alderman in informal talks, other squatters chose a more aggressive approach. 'They blocked my front door at some point. I woke up and could not get out of the house. I managed to escape via the roof and had to call the city hall from my car to ask them to fix it, since I had to rush to an appointment. They sent a carpenter to take the multiplex away. On it, it was written: 'We are closing the door on you. The Calendar Buildings', Duco recalls, while adding that the people responsible for this practical joke were not Jaap and his friends.

Nevertheless, all squatters had difficulty understanding why the city did not want to turn this complex into one of those new art factories the city had promised to develop. So they decided to not leave easily. Eventually about 500 people, probably all of what remained of the Amsterdam squatters movement at that time, fought all night against the police. Bas van de Geyn explains that their anger came from realizing that the policy that was installed for the benefit of their scene, was now used against them. Bas: 'The city had prestigious studio buildings in mind, and aimed at getting big names to rent studios, while the community of the Calendar Buildings was doing exactly what the new art factory policy had intended'. The eviction of the Calendar Buildings had only made the alternative scene more aware of what they wanted to fight for. In hindsight, the attempt to get the buildings legalized and funded through the Art Factory Policy proved understandable, as a few squats, such as OT301, would eventually go through such a procedure.

Given the increasing participation of the (former) squatters in the debate around the art factory policy, a few evenings were organized in Plantage Doklaan in 2004 and 2005. Plantage Doklaan is one of the cultural squats that was legalized and therefore provided the perfect backdrop for a discussion with the city government. The tone of these meetings was a strategic one. The underlying question was how they could get the city back for the subculture they represented. The organizers called themselves De Vrije Ruimte [The Open Space], and among them were the eventual founders of Urban Resort: Hessel Dokkum, Eric Duivenvoorden, Hay Schoolmeesters, Jaap Draaisma, Fred Stammeshaus and Hein de Haan. When the organizers criticized the city's ongoing attempts to set up art factories, alderman Duco Stadig challenged them to set up their own space. During this evening, the idea of finding an empty building and setting up an art factory on their own terms materialized. Shortly after that, Urban Resort was established as a not-for-profit foundation.

· · · · · · · · ·

When the organizers criticized the city's ongoing
attempts to set up art factories, alderman Duco Stadig
challenged them to set up their own space.

· · · · · · · · ·

The former squatters realized they had to find a building and Jaap Schoufour, head of the Art Factory Bureau, suggested the Volkskrant building. Negotiations with the owner of the building took up to six months and the Art Factory Bureau played no part in this except for looking at the rental contract. Jaap recalls they were very keen on the city government not to be included in the Volkskrant building project. 'The deal was to have the owner invest 400.000 euro into our project. Later we came to find out that of this amount, 200.000 euro actually came out of the Art Factory Policy'. At the time however, they were unaware of this. Thinking the only investment came from the owner of the building, Urban Resort decided to take on the challenge.

Over the course of spring 2007, they organized several brainstorm sessions in which they came up with plans for the building. At this time, they did not picture a building that would be dedicated solely to the production of art. In fact, their ideas had much more to do with enabling an alternative way of working, and setting up a community with a certain atmosphere. Rooms for silence and meditation, a therapy practice, a crèche, a technical workshop, kitchens, and even spots for hammocks were on the list of possible uses. Judging from these ideas, it is clear that they had no idea how sought-after every spot of the building would become.

People interested in renting a studio come listen to Jaap Draaisma during an open night.

# Chapter 2

# CASH-STRIPPED BOHEMIA: 2007-2009



On the first of June 2007, the owner of the building, housing corporation Het Oosten, handed over the keys of the building to Urban Resort. Nothing had changed after De Volkskrant newspaper had left its out-dated residence. Bas van de Geyn:

When we entered the building, central heating had not been cut off and lights were still switched on. So we knew that at some point utility bills would start coming in. Although we did not have to pay rent for a few months, we needed to find enough tenants as quickly as possible, so that we could start charging rent after that, and cover our expenses. Luckily, the largest part of the building was made up of small office spaces, which was exactly what self-employed graphic designers, coders, copywriters and the like needed.

‘The mail boxes, tables, cables, kitchen equipment. The journalists
had walked away with nothing more than their papers and PCs’.

When Urban Resort took over, the building looked exactly as the journalists had left it. ‘Everything was there’, Jaap Schoufour from the Art Factory Bureau recalls:

The mail boxes, tables, cables, kitchen equipment. The journalists had walked away with nothing more than their papers and PCs. So when Urban Resort entered the building they could use everything. The first tenants turned mailboxes into cupboards. The first floor had carpet because the board room of De Volkskrant had been there. This added some sort of glamorous element, which was hilarious. The famous Volkskrant-cartoonist Opland had worked on the fifth floor and he had drawn on the walls of his room. Of course, that was kept as it was too.

Most of the floors of the eight story building were already divided into small offices, set up to be used by one or two people. This made the building a perfect place for people who were looking to put a desk and a computer in a room and start working without having to make too many alterations. Although Urban Resort hoped that people would start making the place their own, they soon realized the new generation was not as keen on DIY as they were. 'It is a bit of a culture shock to them. Instead of liking the fact that they can change around their entire floor, the creatives of the new generation think it is a bit of a hassle. They want a floor which is completely ready', Jaap Draaisma said at the time, in an interview with Amsterdam-based newspaper *Het Parool*.[20]

Although the larger part of the building was practically ready to use, there were some odd-sized parts as well. The second floor was where Volkskrant editors wrote their copy. For the sake of quick communication when deadlines were pressing, this area was one big open space of 1500 square meters. The third floor had about seven small darkrooms for press photographs to be developed, which were way too many for even the most dedicated artistic photographer with a preference for analog photography. The basement could be the perfect place to build soundproof recording studios, provided that yet-to-be-found tenants would be willing to invest in constructing those. The top floor, finally, was the newspaper's former company restaurant; a large space offering a majestic view of the city. It was clear that this was the perfect spot for a bar or club of some sort, if only the right license could be arranged.

· · · · · · · ·

It was clear that this was the perfect spot for a bar or club of some
sort, if only the right license could be arranged.

· · · · · · · ·

But none of these practical issues could harm the feeling of excitement that invaded the building as soon as the former squatters took over the place in May of 2007. They had called in the help of Kaos Projects, a group of self-styled anarchist organization experts, who would help out in getting a community of tenants together. One of them was Julien Haffmans. Julien was intrigued by the way in which Jaap and his fellow ex-squatters used the term *vrijplaats*, which translates into English as 'free place', to indicate an autonomous place in the city. Julien: 'At that time, the word *vrijplaats* was used in a negative sense in public discourse to indicate that a place was devoid of rules, full of illegal activity. But free places are places where people can make their own laws, which is a very positive thing'.

The news that there was such a new 'free place' in Amsterdam spread like wildfire. In no time, six hundred people rushed to the empty Volkskrant building, determined to get a workspace there. A first open night was organized. Jaap Draaisma: 'We had sent letters of invitation to the squats and art schools in town, and because of our network and the long waiting lists for studio spaces everywhere else, it did not surprise me that so many people turned up. What did surprise me were the somewhat more commercial types that were drawn to our initiative as well'. Everyone signed up and eventually about two thousand names were on the list for a space at the Volkskrant building. Wondering how to turn such a large and diverse crowd into a reasonably well-composed group of tenants, the former squatters turned to their own heritage. In their squatting days, they had seen that self-managing communities rarely exceeded thirty people. Julien: 'We decided to translate this experience into the present, and said that in order to rent an area or floor in the Volkskrant building, you needed to be a group and you needed to have a clear idea of what you want to achieve here with that group'.



## Good Vibrations

Throughout the summer of 2007, hundreds of strangers walked into the building, with Urban Resort and Kaos Projects welcoming all of them. Usually, people entered the building just to take a look, but the building's new hosts quickly got them to talk about their aspirations. There was something about the attitude of the Volkskrant building's new hosts that made people share their dreams within a few minutes, Julien recalls. 'All we did was say: "Yes! That's exactly what we would like you to do here!" As a result, people felt touched'.

It seemed as if Urban Resort and Kaos Projects had intuitively found a way to transport the radical political attitude of the 80s squatters culture into a contemporary DIY-approach in order to capture the imagination of a diverse crowd of Amsterdammers. The art school students and young creative entrepreneurs who showed up wanting to join the project were, of course, far too young to recall the wild and free days of a quarter century ago. Yet they understood that this emerging space allowed you to do things that you could not do elsewhere. 'People entered the building and said: "I get this, I understand what's going on here"', says Julien. 'Keep in mind that the building still looked like an abandoned newspaper office, and yet people got enthusiastic about it. They would say: "wait, this is like in the 80s!" Or: "wait, this is do-it-yourself!"'.

But from those first individual glimpses of recognition or inspiration to a shared sense of purpose, it was still a long way. People could only become tenants if they applied as a group. The idea behind this requirement was simple: if a group of unrelated individuals would manage to come together and decide on a name and some sort of goal, this could set off a variety of self-management processes. Apart from the ideology, there was a practical side to it as well. Julien: 'Setting up the building one tenant at a time would have been impossible. To begin with, we simply could not remember a thousand names'.

Urban Resort and Kaos Projects were convinced this exercise in self-management would lead to a situation in which these groups would run the building. Jaap Draaisma: 'We thought that certain managerial tasks would be taken up by groups of tenants. We had no intention of doing everything ourselves'. The people from Urban Resort had experienced a high level of self-organization in squats and did not think that paying a small amount of rent would get in the way of active participation. Jaap: 'In a squat you always pay for utilities, plus a small amount for other general expenses. The way I saw it was that with the Volkskrant building, we only increased the amount of money we needed for those general expenses. I did not think it would make a big difference'.



It must have been due to this belief in the self-organizing capacities of their tenants that Urban Resort did not ask people to pay a deposit. 'Granted, that was one of the stupidest things we did', Jaap Draaisma admits. 'You might ask how we could have made that mistake with thirty years of experience in setting up buildings under our belt', he adds. Apparently, the spirit of the 80s had survived, but its organizational form had to be re-invented.

**Mixing & Matching People**
Throughout the summer of 2007, so-called 'dating nights' were organized in the Volkskrant with the aim to introduce interested individuals to groups which were already applying to get a space. The first dating night took place on June 1. A YouTube video of this evening shows Jaap, Hay, and the other initiators of Urban Resort, alongside the people from Kaos Projects, in front of a crowd of potential tenants.[21] Standing on a table in the largest room of the building, Jaap remarks that 'Urban Resort now has this building for the next six years', which is followed by cheers and applause. 'Based on the idea of squatting and self-management, and because we don't want to play landlord, we want groups to rent an entire floor', he continues. After that, already existing groups presented themselves in order to attract more members, a principle of self-organization. 'They stood up on that same table and started telling absolutely fantastic stories about what they were capable of. I remember two women with polka-dotted umbrellas who put on quite a show', Julien remembers.

The spokeswoman of another group said they intended to build, on their floor, a 'multi-functional space in which to organize exhibitions, film screenings, discussion nights, lectures, and courses'.[22] She continued that these would not be exclusively aimed at the Volkskrant building, but also 'open to the outside'. Many initiatives were not just there to find a quiet space to work, but wanted to add something to Amsterdam's cultural life as well. Those evenings were marked by the joy of anticipation. 'We would start around 8 pm, and after the presentations from the group we would party with a DJ and cocktails. The building was one big, buzzing beehive', Jaap Draaisma remembers. After groups were formed, they would go to great lengths to improve their chances of getting their lease. Outside of these evenings, the emerging groups were working hard to ensure a spot as well. Julien:

> We were in the building every day and the most determined people would come in every day as well. They would ask if they would get keys, or whether they could get the spot they had their eyes set on. There was definitely a competition going on between groups and we encouraged them to feel the affluence of possibilities, and tried to foster the growth of commitment to their own dreams.

After groups had been formed, the issue of dividing space appeared. Julien:

> If we knew people would not be able to pay for one of the regular office spaces, we would take them to the sixth floor, which had odd-sized spaces, and say "just look what you could do with this!". Most people wanted a space of their own but we asked whether they would be up for sharing a studio. Or we would take them up to the second floor, where the option of sharing a space was more feasible because the spaces still had to be created, and we would say: "look at that beautiful light coming from all sides through the windows!".

Jelmer Rypkema, a landscape designer, was one of these people. He would eventually rent his own workspace on the second floor but at first wanted the second floor to stay one big open space. 'I wanted to use it as a shared studio space big enough for all sorts of equipment and machines, with little corners for individual use. I will keep making gardens, you know, but in the end, it is what I do to make rent. I thought, what if I could do something with painting? For me it was about the opportunity to develop myself'.

· · · · · · · ·

'The building was one big, buzzing beehive'.

· · · · · · · ·

As the processes of finding spaces, and allies to share them with, took the entire summer, some groups simply dispersed. Those with the stamina to stay together over such a long period of time tried to get as much space as they could. Julien:

> These groups were all saying they were bigger than they actually were. Instead of arguing with them, we were very affirmative and said: "yes, of course you'll make it happen". At the same time, we had to get them to share their space with another group. So Jan Gieszen, my colleague, came up with the brilliant idea of saying that the building was elastic, that its walls would expand to accommodate all.

Erjee Vroling was part of a group that received such a message. Erjee is a graphic designer who was so eager to get a place in the building for him and his friends that he postponed his own graduation from art school in order to work on the plan for his group. He remembers, quite vividly, the method Kaos Projects applied. 'They made us do some exercises, they would ask us things like "what if you are all standing around a swimming pool, would you dare jump in together"?. It was some weird stuff, but all I was thinking was that I wanted a place in the building'.

While Kaos Projects believed that group dynamics would do their work, and the community could take shape organically, it also became apparent that the Volkskrant building project had to deal with some serious practical problems that needed active management. One of those problems was the fact that the floor plans of the building the previous owner had provided were inapt. Urban Resort asked their friend Bas van de Geyn to measure the surface of all floors. Bas, at the time a recent graduate in social geography, started off with a mixture of enthusiasm and amazement. 'I did not know anything about property development', he recounts. 'I really just started out with an ordinary tape measure, because I did not even know that there was equipment for this. Tenants had joined the Volkskrant building in that DIY atmosphere, so some had measured their space themselves. I then had to arrange meetings and measuring sessions with them to see if our numbers matched'.



· · · · · · · ·



· · · · · · · ·

Even with the difficulty of this task aside, his first impressions of the overall Volkskrant building project were quite overwhelming. Bas: 'There was this little office behind the reception that everyone from Urban Resort and Kaos Projects worked at. That room was packed all the time. There was an enormous vibe going on. I remember thinking, "hopefully we'll manage to keep this going"'. It was the financial precarity of the whole situation that was the largest threat. Bas: 'One week into the project I already saw that the whole thing could easily be over in a few weeks' time'.

Practical issues did not keep tenants-to-be from starting to make use of the building. In June 2007, the top floor was used for the rehearsal of a theater performance by theatre group Opium voor het Volk [Opium for the People]. The space used to be the staff restaurant of De Volkskrant and would later turn into the popular spot Canvas. But at this point, not many things had changed since the journalists had moved out. 'Even those small containers you keep the sandwich meats in were still there', one of the audience members recalled.

Nevertheless, many organizational issues were pending. The two main issues were the lack of manpower on the side of Urban Resort and the absence of even the most basic administrative system. In the early days, Hay Schoolmeesters was often the only one from Urban Resort who was at the Volkskrant building full time. 'I worked all day in that small office and rebuilt old filing systems of previous projects to create some sort of administrative system. I did not go home. I slept at the Volkskrant building in a sleeping bag. Every now and then, Jaap would tell me to go and shower because we had an appointment at the city hall', Hay recalls.

The first rent would be due on the first day of November 2007, so the pressure was on to have the building full of paying tenants by then. In order to achieve this, all sorts of mundane yet crucial tasks had to be ticked off the list. Urban Resort was given a huge box full of keys without labels; each was supposed to give access to one of the work spaces. Hay's partner, Caï van Hoboken, had a good eye for recognizing keys' shapes and spent days matching key sets to doors. The group around Erjee Vroling, who was introduced before as a participant in the swimming pool exercise, moved into the fifth floor and started building an entrance from the staircase to their hallway. The fourth floor was taken by a group of artists who demolished one of the two toilet sections in order to build their own kitchen. The second floor was still an open space but, awaiting permission to build walls, people had started to mark their own sections using laundry line and bunting. Those tenants finally decided to divide the big open space into small studios. Jelmer Rypkema participated in this. 'We built all those walls out of plaster in a week. It was quite impressive to see how much we could achieve together', he says.

**Spending Cash**
While the working spaces were coming together, there was an increasing financial problem. In the beginning, Urban Resort aimed to charge 80% of its studio spaces with the lowest possible rent. But this soon turned out to be unfeasible. Furthermore, since the art factory had started off without actual rental contracts, because the measurements of spaces were still pending, some tenants took the liberty of not paying rent. Bas: 'We had given everyone an estimation of what their rent was likely to be, and asked them to set this sum aside on a monthly basis until we would be able to charge the rent in retrospect. This worked remarkably well for the majority of tenants, but there were exceptions'. One of these was the third floor.

· · · · · · · ·

While the working spaces were coming together, there was an
increasing financial problem.

· · · · · · · ·

The third floor had formed a collective and a few people were responsible for collecting and paying rent on behalf of everyone. Fatumoh Farah, one of the few tenants left from those days, recalls their initial plans. 'We had a general meeting every fortnight and some budget for activities and expenses. But then people just refused to pay rent. I think they did not realize they had to show commitment to the group'. Jaap Draaisma: 'Many of those tenants from the third floor were being screwed over by the leaders of their collective. This caused them, and us, great financial trouble. Finally, in the spring of 2008, we had to decide to kick out those who did not pay'. Outstanding bills remained an issue until 2010. Jaap Schoufour remembers the many meetings he had in 2008 and 2009 with Urban Resort concerning the financial troubles. 'I was always astonished with the stories they told me. Some people seemed convinced that they did not have to pay rent. I really saw how hard Urban Resort worked. And they didn't even make any money from it either'. Jaap Draaisma, however, emphasizes the fun that characterized the first and indeed challenging period of the Volkskrant building art factory. 'The first half year was fantastic. Having so much space, all that opportunity, and parties everywhere thrown by people who were starting up their studio'. Despite the practical hiccups and hard work, there was a sense of excitement and positivity on the side of Urban Resort.

What eventually saved the building from bankruptcy was a trick Hay came up with. 'We called it "operation carwash"', he recounts. 'We blocked all key cards, so no one could access the building on their own. We set up office in the entrance hall, simply by putting about seven tables out there. Everyone who came in was screened to see if they had any outstanding bills. If so, they had to pay immediately or else they were denied entrance. Some of us stood up behind the tables, in case things got violent. Eventually, the tenants who had paid joined us out of curiosity'. Six of these 'car washes' happened; most of them during office hours and some of them at night to catch those who had been avoiding them.

**The First Outbursts of Creativity**
In spite of the continuing financial distress, the Volkskrant building quickly became a place for intense creative production and wacky celebrations of all things less mainstream. It had its official opening as an art factory on September 21, 2007. The borough originally did not grant the license for the party, but by the intervention of the mayor the party was able to go on. In line with the atmosphere of excitement, this fact was celebrated with a big party throughout the entire building. In line with the policy of admitting groups, rather than individuals, different networks started to settle down and grow in and around the building. The first two years in the life of the new creative hub were characterized by a very diverse set of initiatives, all marked by a buzz of creativity and the feeling that everyone was there to make the place into more than the sum of its parts. Only a few days after the official opening, some tenants seamlessly linked the fact that they were finally able to enter their workspaces to the Soviet space program. 'We are going into (our) space! This calls for a challenge and a festive manifestation, Cosmic Party, to celebrate the 40th anniversary of the Russian satellite Sputnik One going into space', read the invite of their party.

· · · · · · · ·

What eventually saved the building from bankruptcy was a trick Hay
came up with. 'We called it "operation carwash"'.

· · · · · · · ·

Furthermore the first so-called Volksevent was held in November 2007. With generous funding from the Amsterdam Arts Fund, awarded with the building barely up and running, Urban Resort was able to organize a monthly event showcasing the work of their residents and offering a platform for interaction and celebration. Each month, another floor was responsible for hosting the event and the funding was used as an initial catalyst, with the hope that each floor would subsequently start to organize it themselves. In January 2008 it was the turn of Volksspectrum, the community on the third floor which neglected paying rent. In spite of these problems, they did organize an event with great food, childcare, and percussion performances, showing that even though some initial communities of the Volkskrant building fell apart, they did have some fun in the meantime. The Volksevents were organized until 2009, the duration during which funding was available, but discontinued due to a lack of commitment on the side of tenants, illustrating how tricky it can be to create self-sustainable organizational processes with no financial support.



The first two years in the life of the new creative hub were
characterized by a very diverse set of initiatives, all marked by a
buzz of creativity and the feeling that everyone was there to make
the place into more than the sum of its parts.





In an article which appeared in *Amsterdam Weekly*, an art management professional tells them that the building is 'really good for people who come from outside the country and haven't really got a network in Amsterdam yet'.[23] Its international appeal was indeed one of the strongest features of the Volkskrant building art factory, especially in its first years. If a city's success is indeed dependent on the input it gets from talented and creative professionals, as is suggested by, for instance, the sociologist Saskia Sassen,[24] then the Volkskrant building provided a strong and easy-to-handle tool for this. Many artists who came from other countries described how easy it was to join the building, even without becoming tenants, as long as they knew people who were looking for someone to sublet their space to for a while, or share a studio with. As such, the building acted as an informal and light-weight residency program, given that the formal structures aimed at the same objectives are often constrained by the restrictive hierarchies of the contemporary art world.

Illustrative of the role of the Volkskrant building as an informal residency program, or incubator space, is an article in the German weekly magazine *Der Spiegel* featuring the Volkskrant building. Volkskrant building resident Dorien Westphal states here: 'I am a nomad. If it's not buzzing any more where I live, I'll be gone fast', Dorien tells the reporter.[25] Westphal, a product designer, has a 30 square meter studio on the fourth floor of the building and gained worldwide success, making handbags out of bicycle tires and inflatable mattresses, through her contacts in Amsterdam. But Amsterdam's biggest appeal, she tells *Der Spiegel*, has to be the Volkskrant building. 'With almost a hundred like-minded people, she is building a self-organizing collective. This colorful group has taken over this building for seven years. A painter piles up his work in the corridor, a wood artist drags a sawing machine into his space',[26] describes the German magazine. Even when the Volkskrant building was not the main topic, it got a lot of attention from the press due to the fact that its tenants were doing interesting things. In March 2008, daily local newspaper *Het Parool* praised the musical skills of Volkskrant building tenant and DJ Steven de Peven, who would go on to organize many club evenings at Canvas, the club on the top of floor of the building.[27] One month later, hip hop act La Melodia, who had only just settled into the building, was interviewed by magazine *LiveXS*.[28] Already in 2007, a group of artists from the fourth floor set up the Klik Animation Festival. It started out slowly but would eventually grow into an internationally recognized platform for animation art.

Planet Art, a curatorial initiative that took residency on the ground floor of the Volkskrant building, managed to attract a lot of attention with their events and exhibitions. One of the first shows they curated had an old fashioned gaming machine as its focal point, and they followed this up with an exhibition with activist video art about immigration and their very own punk art festival, Gogbot, among many other things. But the most attention they received was without a doubt when Tinkerbell, a young Dutch artist, exhibited at Planet Art in October 2008. Made out of dead animals, her artworks caused quite the stir. 'Simonse's work is all about exposing the hypocrisy in people's interaction with animals, particularly their domestic pets: kids treat them like fashion accessories. Along with all the hate mail, her stunts have also earned her guest spots on Dutch TV and a sizable share of international press', the Amsterdam branch of *Time Out Magazine* wrote,[29] while *Het Parool* reported that Planet Art was expecting 'raging animal activists'.[30]

In December of that same year, another tenant of the Volkskrant building made his claim to fame. Tom Trago had been an upcoming DJ for a few years already, playing sets in many of Amsterdam's respected nightclubs. He had been hesitating to record his own album because he was afraid to give up his spots at Paradiso and Jimmy Woo, two renowned clubs in Amsterdam, but also realized he needed to develop his own sound in order to grow. Having his own studio at the Volkskrant building allowed Tom to work on his music for a year straight. 'I had to calm down a bit, question myself and gain the confidence that I could do my own thing', he said about this period.

*Voyage Direct*, the album resulting from his period of secluded labor won De Grote Prijs van Nederland [The Netherlands' Big Prize], a prestigious national music award. It would not take long before he would be booked to play sets all over the world, from Ibiza to the United States. At the time of research for this book, in 2013, Tom Trago would be traveling abroad at least twice a week and said that the reason he was still based in Amsterdam was because it was 'conveniently located for world travel'. Although he certainly holds the credits to this success, having an inexpensive studio space on a floor which he shared with friends did help.

Another success the building helped nurture is the artistic collective Pips:lab. Although the group had existed eight years prior to the opening of the art factory, the fact that some of its members had a studio space in the Volkskrant building did help their collective practices. In May of 2009, the collective hosted what Het Parool described as 'a musical playground'[31] in the, by then defunct, headquarters of Dutch newspaper *Trouw*, conveniently located opposite to the Volkskrant building. During this event, visitors were invited to use installation works, creating rhythms or drawing with light. The Volkskrant building was also at the intersection of events less artistic, yet nevertheless very social. On December 13th, 2008 the building hosted the 'No Mercy Supply International Weed Cup', a marijuana contest. Among its jury members was hippy poet Simon Vinkenoog, no stranger to some of the founding members of Urban Resort. 'Just stay cool, high, and take time to fly!', the flyer read encouragingly.

It is this mixture of underground tendencies, with cutting-edge experimental art, and commercially viable music, that best defined the first two years of the Volkskrant building. Yet in spite of its alternative characteristics, the Volkskrant building soon started to appeal to a broad audience. A massive factor in this was Canvas, the club and restaurant on the top floor, which would attract visitors from as far as New York. We delve into the role the venue played in the success of the Volkskrant building in more detail in the next chapter.

· · · · · · · ·

In spite of its alternative characteristics, the Volkskrant building soon
started to appeal to a broad audience.

· · · · · · · ·



### The Flip Side of Openness

Looking back at the first two and a half years of the Volkskrant building, we can conclude that in some respects, the building was indeed a 'free place' of sorts. As a result, the place also attracted people who had nowhere else to go. 'Free zones attract damaged people', Julien says. 'One of our rules was that we welcomed everyone. Well, I learned that there is a lot of trauma amongst the people who are looking for freedom', she adds. In some cases it was hard to recognize the difference between a high level of creativity and serious mental illness. One of those cases was a young German man. Julien recalls meeting him just like she met everyone in those days, by asking them what they were dreaming of. 'He was just very sensitive, poetic, musically gifted, intelligent, but a bit lost. In hindsight I think he was already psychotic then', Julien recalls.

> Because he was homeless, we gave him a place on the sixth floor where he could stay. He was a musician, and an extremely talented one according to his friends. But during the first year it became clear he was not taking good care of himself. He did not eat well, abused drugs, and at a certain point he was just full on psychotic. I finally took him to my GP to get him medication, and we found his parents in Germany.

A second case she recalls was a homeless person who was friends with one of the tenants who had been an active member of the Volkskrant building community from the early stages. His case was different, because he was not officially given a space, but stayed in the building for a couple of weeks nevertheless. Julien:

He came from Greece and had worked as a roadie, I believe. He had found himself a place in the basement where he could spend the night, but did not sleep at all. Instead, he was roller skating through the corridors of the building with a crown of LED-lights on his head. Or he went to the top floor, where Canvas had just started up, and started heating up chickens in their oven and cleaning up tables. He did strange, but fun, things. In a way he was also guarding the place.

Apart from not being a tenant officially, there did not seem to be a big problem at first. 'Well', says Julien, 'he had "friends" over in the basement and at some point hard drugs were found in the space he used. Urban Resort suspected he was dealing and kicked him out. A few weeks later, we came to learn he had committed suicide. We felt a kind of awkward responsibility there, since it turned out we had somehow taken care of him collectively, but had not *really* taken care of him'.

### Giving in to Security

The openness that characterized the early days of the Volkskrant building was not just an openness towards all kinds of people. It was also a literal lack of closed doors, resulting in theft. Some offices had all their computers stolen, and the coffee vending machine on the ground floor was broken into a few times. Hella Masuger, one of the first tenants and head of a foundation, had her office broken into as well. 'I don't think it is a secure environment here', she says in a short video the Art Factory Bureau made about the matter.[32] The large scale and chaotic nature of the building were not the only explanations for theft. Rents were kept as low as possible and this meant that hiring security would lead to an increase in rent. Quite in the vein of the overall project, the lack of security instigated several DIY initiatives among tenants. The fifth floor, for instance, built a wall and door to prevent entrance to their floor. Erjee Vroling: 'Urban Resort kept postponing that, so we did it ourselves. When they saw it, they said it did not comply with regulations, but of course we didn't care'.

Obviously, the issue of theft is not exclusive to the Volkskrant building. It points towards one of the paradoxes, that can be found more often, of creative production in urban spaces. Creative production of whatever kind cannot exist without a good degree of openness. The nature of the modes of production happening in spaces such as the Volkskrant building needs unexpected triggers in order to thrive, and one of these is informal encounters between people. This is the reason why every self-respecting operator of a creative hub, or co-working space, mentions openness in their mission statement. But as soon as creative production requires valuable equipment, things get a bit tricky. How open can a building be before creatives have their gear stolen? While security might be an unpleasant issue to deal with for people with a rather libertarian predisposition; for ex-squatters it is a real pain.

After several severe instances of theft, Urban Resort had to come up with a response. Pantar, an organization offering work experience to unemployed people, was willing to offer their people as receptionists. In addition, Urban Resort limited tenants' access to their own floors only.

Although it made the place safer, it was not really helping the openness and serendipitous nature of the building. Finally, theft also led to a decrease in an atmosphere where tenants could still run into each other. Fatumoh Farah: 'We had all our computers stolen. Somehow, after those incidents, the trust was gone. People started to mind only their own business'.

**Onwards & Upwards**

In spite of its initial hiccups, the Volkskrant building remained a place that attracted attention. So much so, that the city council realized how much the art factory represented the creative image of Amsterdam. Urban Resort received around a hundred requests over the years from city hall to show around foreign groups of officials. 'They came from everywhere: Kazakhstan, Russia, Germany, you name it', Jaap remembers.

> They were invited, of course, because Amsterdam officials were loving the building too. It was a raw place, but also comfortable somehow, because they knew me and they knew the city supported it. Foreign groups would also run into people from their own country, which was, again, great for the international appeal of Amsterdam. The daughter of then-mayor of Amsterdam, Job Cohen, even celebrated her birthday at Canvas.

But the highlight must have been the time Jaap had to free a lift full of civil servants at 3 am. 'They had hired out Canvas for a function and continued partying in the lift, I think', Jaap says.

There seems to be an odd poetic justice to the fact that the same city that had once evicted places such as Wijers was now actively subsidizing a somewhat similar initiative.[33] It was doing so both through the official channels and by having their functions there. Jaap: 'Indeed, they embraced the very thing they wanted to rid themselves of. This embrace also had to do with the fact that we were one of the first ones offering a solution for all these vacant buildings. There was nothing alternative about that, it was just smart'. But it was not until several years of the art factory's first steps towards fame, that it would become clear exactly how smart their choice for this building had been.

During the Transvormers Festival, one of the tenants presented a project in which she invited visitors to help her bring the model building she had built to life.

# NETWORKS OF CREATIVE PRODUCTION: 2009-2013

Urban Resort did their best to match the squatters' ethos of autonomy with the wishes of the new creative class and to play by the rules and regulations of the city council. Doing this meant to shift from looking at things in terms of of 'what is best' to 'what works in which context'. Although initiated by squatters, the Volkskrant building did not become very squat-like. One of the most obvious reasons for this was the fact that rent had to be charged. 'The big difference between this place and a squat is that when you squat, you don't have to pay rent. And when you don't have to pay rent, you don't have to work. That means you have a lot of time to set things up together, organize stuff', as one of the tenants put it. Jaap Schoufour, head of the Art Factory Bureau, put it in the following words: 'The start of the Volkskrant building was way too ideological. Urban Resort copied their experiences from the 80s into 2007'.

## No Formula for Success

Doreen Wittenbols, who works at Urban Resort's financial department, but also used to live at the Plantage Doklaan, one of Amsterdam's legalized squats, confirms the fundamental difference between living and working in such a place, and working in an art factory. She thinks that the basis on which a squat functions does not translate well into the current context. 'Much of the public funding for young artists has disappeared now, and artists have never earned much to begin with. When we talk about how we want them to contribute to the community of the Volkskrant building I sometimes wonder: what can we expect from them? In a squatted community people simply have more time to do things for the collective, and it does not work that way here', she says. Hay Schoolmeesters acknowledges this:

It took a long time before we realized that by asking rent from the people we provided with space, they would participate less as a result. In squatted communities, your participation is a necessity, because there are always things that need to be done in order to keep the building. Here in the Volkskrant building people think: "I pay rent, therefore I can expect some things in return". We must be aware of that, and as an organization we should spend more time interacting with our tenants.

The only strategy for this, he thinks, is not giving up. 'You have to continue to organize meetings and parties. Who cares if no one shows up? Next time they will. And if not, the time after that. That's the only way to do it. Just continue to create a good atmosphere, and never give up'. In spite of Hay's and others' good intentions, the self-managing communities Urban Resort had envisioned did not take off in the way they had hoped. All but two of the initial groups dissolved, in the sense that they did not become self-organizing groups who paid rent on behalf of the entire group, took on maintenance tasks, and organized events. On top of that, the planned interaction across floors was constrained by the fact that tenants could only access their own floor.

At the same time, many of the tenants of the dissolved groups did stay. The original group Oostblok, artists who resided in the back wing of the second floor, hosted activist initiatives against the regeneration plans for the immediate area. Fashion journalist and performer Aynouk Tan became a tenant in the building as part of a fashion collective. While their collective plans did not take off, Aynouk built a name for herself with a thought-provoking column in the quality newspaper *NRC Handelsblad*. Having remained in the building throughout the years, she argued for the importance of alternative places when she was interviewed by Amsterdam's local television station AT5.[34] Such examples show that even though the original setup with self-managing groups failed, some of its alternative spirit continued to mark the building.

Looking at the period after the initial two year startup phase, it is fairly obvious that the Volkskrant building became a relevant and important place for the creative scene, as well as the young crowds of the city. Although rent was increased several times due to all sorts of unforeseen costs, people were still dying to get a place in the building. Some even entered floors without permission, knocking on studio doors to ask tenants for advice on how to get a studio space. So, if self-management did not work out, what did? What made the Volkskrant building successful in its own way, and what did this success look like?

Despite the claims of consultants, the desires of policymakers, and the rhetoric of overenthusiastic trend watchers, there is no formula for a successful creative hub, or, indeed, art factory. In fact, the very idea of such a formula begs the question of what success should actually look like. As discussed in the previous chapters, the art factory in the Volkskrant building started to look very different from the spaces and practices imagined by the people setting it up. Yet again, in this process of trial and error, a lot of things happened and a lot of fun was had. In this chapter we delve into what we think are the key ingredients that made the Volkskrant building what it was: the venue on the top floor, the fact that people could alter the spaces they used, and the sociality that characterized the atmosphere of the building. This sociality did lead to some interesting collaborations, but we argue that this should not be seen as the central purpose of a place such as the Volkskrant building. We will also show how each of these elements cannot be seen as exclusively 'bottom-up' or 'top-down', to borrow again from the ubiquitous lingo of creativity consultants. In order to illustrate this, we will finish with an example of an annual festival that was organized in the building. But we will start with Canvas, undoubtedly one of the biggest contributors to the art factory's success.

## Canvas: Parties and a Great View

As was the case with many elements of the Volkskrant building, Canvas was a result of chance combined with some initial good selection. Thijs Timmers was barely out of art school when he started looking for a studio to paint, and ended up at the Volkskrant building. Initially part of the group that took on the fifth floor, he soon came to learn that Urban Resort was looking for an entrepreneur to turn the top floor, the former staff restaurant, into a cafe of some sort. 'At that point I had been making cocktails for festivals on the side for some time', Thijs recalls, while being interviewed on the Canvas terrace. 'I think my plan was chosen because my concept was based on the participation of other tenants besides me'. Without a loan from the bank, and with very few resources, he started out in the summer of 2007.

· · · · · · · ·



· · · · · · · ·

Canvas, as the name suggests, would be a space open for the exhibition of artwork and the showcasing of musical talent. As the interior consisted of rotating artworks, such as tables painted by artists, the place would undergo a metamorphosis from time to time. Although a full license was pending for the first six months after its unofficial opening, Thijs did what he could to cater to the new residents of the building. 'I would walk through the corridors of each floor with trolleys in order to sell dinner to the new tenants. It was difficult though, because many of the studios were still to be rented out'.

What did work well were the parties that were soon being thrown: fashion events for emerging designers, a theme night centered around music from a particular year, or a party dedicated to girls smoking cigars. Sometimes party goers were invited to dress up in vintage clothes lent to them by the creative duo Visjuweel. 'Our motivation is to see how people, once in fancy dress, become much more liberated. In different clothes, it seems people can let go completely', the duo said to *Het Parool* in December 2008.[35] Of course, Canvas benefited massively from the DJs who were Thijs Timmers' friends. In the first few years, Tom Trago, also part of the fifth floor network that introduced Thijs to the building, would play his sets in exchange for free food and drink. Artist Steven de Peven and party organizer Silvester Pöll, both tenants downstairs, would conceptualize and plan the themes and entertainment for many nights. And of course, the place had solid assets such as great cocktails and a fantastic roof top terrace.

Next to clubbing, Canvas' restaurant did not go unnoticed either, although it seems not many people came for the food. The food critic of *nrc.next* wrote in the fall of 2008 that Canvas was 'a spot to look at other people' and that 'no people in suits had been spotted yet',[36] indicating that the underground vibe was one of its charms. However, Canvas appeared to be not far enough off the beaten track for *The New York Times* not to notice it. In April of 2009 the newspaper wrote that 'Canvas boasts one of the most spectacular and unimpeded views of Amsterdam' and concluded that 'sitting outside with a coffee and a good book is an inspiring way to spend an afternoon'.[37]

With a small interruption in the spring of 2008, when the council closed the club due to complaints from neighbors using the pending license as leverage, Canvas had a straight and steep rise to stardom. 'On a Friday we have about a hundred people for dinner and on a club night we have around 400 guests', said Thijs Timmers by 2012. 'Those big numbers on a club night immediately means that the percentage of tenants among our guests probably does not exceed twenty percent', Thijs readily admitted. From his initial plan to become some sort of living room with extras, Canvas grew into one of the favorite spots for Amsterdammers and visitors for a coffee or a beer with a great view over the city.

Latte-sipping crowds aside, Canvas did maintain its ties with Amsterdam's alternative heritage. Living Legends, an evening showcasing hippie stars from days gone by, was an initiative organized by artist Steven de Peven. The plan emerged completely organically and without Urban Resort's interference. Nevertheless, Jaap Draaisma was pleased and surprised in equal measure to see the alternative crowd that was the precursor of the squatting movement of the 80s, pass by. 'All of a sudden, hippie-artists such as Hans Plomp and Simon Vinkenoog were performing their poetry at Canvas on a Friday night', he recalls. And the Living Legends night was not the only tie to the old hippies and Provos the Volkskrant building had. Willem de Ridder, Fluxus artist and well known member of Amsterdam's 1970s hippie scene, broadcast a radio show from the Volkskrant building for a while. Urban Resort founder Eric Duivenvoorden published a book on the legacy of Provo leader Robert Jasper Grootveld, which was launched at Canvas, and when Robert passed away in 2009, the after party of the funeral took place at the Volkskrant building.

**The Business of Using Space**
The seven remaining floors, together about 10,000 square meters of usable surface, was comprised of the studios and offices of roughly three hundred people from the cultural and creative sector, as well as some non-profit organizations and the occasional accountant or consultant. It was a second - and sometimes clandestine first - home to painters, musicians, sound engineers, dance teachers, writers, internet startups, graphic designers, project managers, computer coders, communication experts, social enterprises, and filmmakers. On an average day, one was likely to run into several dogs and catch the occasional breeze of maijuana in the hallways. The building was accessible for tenants 24/7, making it perfect for after-parties in art studios on the weekends. While you could notice at least an awareness of office hours on most floors, the basement and fifth floor, mostly filled with musicians and artists, were most productive at night.

Throughout the entire building, about a third of all workspaces had their doors open. During the first two years, the larger spaces had been used for events and exhibitions, until Urban Resort needed extra income and started renting them out as lecture halls. Tenants could still use these spaces against a very low hourly rate but now they were regularly used by the Amsterdam University of Applied Sciences. This arrangement caused the building to be invaded by freshmen from time to time. Although some tenants got annoyed with the queues of students in front of 'their' toilets, the scene of young female students readjusting their headscarves and carefully applying eye makeup offered a miniature of Amsterdam's multicultural life.



These encounters aside, the physical setup of the building did not exactly stimulate contact between people. Most of this had to do with the lack of budget. Urban Resort did have not enough money to sacrifice square meters to create communal areas or coffee corners. Some of the common tricks in setting up incubators, such as employing a host or matchmaker, were frowned upon by Urban Resort. While today's community managers might shake their head in disbelief, the lack of these professional social engineers was quite possibly one of the great advantages of the Volkskrant building. This was a place where people were treated like grownups, perfectly able to create and sustain professional social networks on their own if they felt like it. The matchmaking of current co-working spaces was totally absent from this space and it was, of course, the old squatters attitude that kept infantile management techniques out: 'Managing interaction? No way! People have to do it themselves' is what Urban Resort thought most of the time. This attitude was not just one of reluctance, but one of ideology too. Incubators or accelerators for startup companies always keep in mind that the businesses they host should generate profits, and fast; whereas the idea of Urban Resort was always to provide a space outside of the pressures of 'capitalist society'.

This meant not only that tenants were left to their own devices when it came to getting to know one another, but also that they were given a lot of freedom to do with their spaces whatever they wanted. Some tenants created a sort of living room in the corridors of their floor. One of them was Harry Monée, who resided on the second floor. This all-Amsterdam retired butcher collected secondhand organs (the musical instrument, that is) and pianos. Naturally, his talent spilled over into a keen eye for secondhand furniture, and his old-fashioned taste had acquired a vintage quality that was approved of by his neighbor hipster-artists. The fourth floor had taken out a toilet block in its entirety, already in 2007, in order to construct a communal kitchen including a large table, loads of kitchen equipment, and notes put up everywhere on how to use and clean them. Until they would have to move out of their studios in July 2013, this kitchen would serve as the social center of this floor. And of course, many social get-togethers across different floors would continue the party upstairs at Canvas.

Although the setup of the building was less than ideal, listening to the stories of tenants made it clear that simply having a space of one's own to work in often gave them a push in what they were doing. Take app developers Somehow, who had a spacious office on the first floor:

> We painted this place, we invested time. We were so happy with the office and we were here all the time. After one year we realized that although it is great to have this place, we do not need to be here all the time. We now see it as a space to invite people to, for instance, at the beginning of a project. Everyone talks about the network society, but we did not know how to manage these networks. Now, by using this place cleverly, we know it.

Or take Wouter Brandenburg, a music producer and sound engineer whom the building enabled to become a proper professional: 'People from the building asked me to master records for them. I could start an official company, meet up with contacts at Canvas, and use one of the meeting rooms in the building to pitch to investors'. Anne-Marije Poorter, who ran a small production company for theater and music productions on the second floor, says she feels proud to belong to the Volkskrant building when walking into the building. 'I live nearby and have a parking spot for my car here, which also makes me feel more part of everything here. A while ago, I picked some blackberries which grew next to the parking area, and made them into jam. In a way I think that symbolized my ties to this place', she adds. Other tenants had more pedestrian reasons for being part of the Volkskrant community. Esma Linnemann, a freelance journalist, tells us about the feeling of solidarity she gets from the sound of a sewing machine coming from somewhere in the building when she has to work on the weekend to keep a deadline. 'To me, that is the ultimate comfort; to know that other people are working too'.

### DIY on the Fifth Floor

Despite its suboptimal architectural setup, and the reluctance of Urban Resort to manage communities, many people did meet by chance and wonderful collaborations did come out of this. Take for instance Ellis Biemans, who designs fashion, and her partner Erjee Vroling, a graphic designer and DJ. They had a studio on the fifth floor from the beginning in 2007. In 2012, they teamed up with newbie Jasper Eustace, an architect who had relocated from Spain back to the Netherlands and managed to infiltrate the fifth floor's tight network and find himself a workspace there. The three of them started a company whose core business came about 'thanks to this building', as Ellis puts it. Jasper: 'In 2011 we had a cold winter, and at the same time the government cut the WIK [social benefits for underemployed young artists]. Ellis came up with the idea of importing traditional fur boots from Russia as a fashion item, so I joined her and Erjee in that plan'. Six months later, the boots were launched with a hip party in the cutting-edge fashion shop SPRMKT. Dutch newspaper *NRC Handelsblad* published a feature article on the joint endeavors of Ellis, Erjee and Jasper, in which they stated that 'we are creative, so we are fixing it ourselves'.[38] DIY was alive and well, at least as far as the Volkskrant building was concerned.

When wondering what made the Volkskrant building work, the story of the Russian boots does not stand on its own. From 2007 onwards, Erjee and Ellis had been part of a group of young and ambitious artists who would become the creative DNA of the building. DJ Tom Trago and

Thijs Timmers, who have both been mentioned before, belong to the same group, and Ella Gil, who runs the performance collective Curious Behaviour, is another central node of this network. She recalls how the group originally came together. 'Erjee was my flat mate and I asked him to collaborate with me for my graduation project. He then came to learn about the Volkskrant building and asked me to help him put together a group of people to apply for a space. I knew all the others, because almost everyone is from the same art school, the HKU', she explains.

Asked what defines their group, Erjee explains that it has to do with like-mindedness more than anything else. 'In order for an art factory to work out, people have to be like-minded. We have a lot of diversity in terms of professions, but we just understand each other', he says. He also illustrates how the opposite can be true: 'Some years back a few charity organizations rented space here on this floor too. They had more of a 9-to-5 mentality, so we sometimes clashed with them. About what? Well, we are young creatives with a preference for nightlife'. Needless to say, from time to time, this preference reflected in the tidiness of the floor and the amount of empty beer cans present. Nevertheless, a fondness of partying is definitely not all that's keeping them together. Erjee:

> We are still very close as a group because we see that we have a shared interest. Our philosophy is that you have to have a social attitude; talk to one another, share stuff. We select new tenants together. One of the people who recently moved in was a bit hesitant when he noticed that we came into his studio for a chat; he really had to get used to that. Now he has and is really participating, because he sees it just works.

• • • • • • • •

Over the years, the building's social fabric was
made of networks of friends.

• • • • • • • •

Over the years, the building's social fabric was made of networks of friends rather than self-managing groups. The building could be criticized for being too 'in-crowd', yet at the same time it had a surprising number of tenants who had come from other countries to study at art schools or further themselves creatively in other ways. Because of Urban Resort's preference to accept new tenants who already had contacts in the building, newcomers sometimes had an advantage in the sense that they did not have to beat a years-long waiting list made up entirely of locals. As long as you knew someone who already was a tenant, it was easy to become a subletter of someone's studio for a few months, then make friends and move on within the building. In a way, because of its international character, the building's communities bore a resemblance to the international spirit that marked the beginning of the squatting movement as well.

The draw for people from abroad was one aspect in which the Volkskrant building continued the legacy of the squatting days; another was the many activist initiatives that were connected to the building. In the light of culture - and creativity - driven urban regeneration, it had always been easier to frame the Volkskrant building as a creative place, but the fact is that it was also a political one. In 2008, the international peace day, organized by NGO Pax Christi, was held at the Volkskrant building with Bert Koenders, the current Dutch foreign minister, as a keynote speaker. Non-profit organization Privacy First held many events and symposia at the building and other non-profits fighting for the rights of homeless youth (Stichting Zwerfjongeren Nederland), Somali migrants (Stichting Hirda) and sex workers (Voices of Women) had an office in the building. Urban Resort also continued to advise and help new and remaining squats in Amsterdam and was connected to many activist initiatives, such as the Global Uprisings conference in November 2013.

Although many stated that they liked the atmosphere of the building and were interested in what their neighbors did, when it came down to it, most of the Volkskrant building's tenants were simply in search of a space to work. The interactions in the building were mainly social in nature: people borrowed each other's equipment or shared a coffee. In the best instances, they could help each other out. Designers and artists of different stripes could show each other the ropes to editing and layout software. Only in a few lucky cases, for instance for those DJing or designing for Canvas, the building actually provided them with more work opportunities.

· · · · · · · ·



· · · · · · · ·

Creative city officials think about spaces like the Volkskrant building as hot spots where synergies are created and innovation spurred for the sake of generating creative business ventures. However, many collaborations at the Volkskrant building were incidental and not primarily intended to generate substantial income. Rather, they facilitated social exchanges that would otherwise not have happened, or were done for the sake of plain fun. Nadine Faber, for example, is an emerging artist who came to the Volkskrant building in June 2012 in search of the right atmosphere. 'I like being autonomous but being part of something at the same time', Nadine explains. 'I know most of the people in this hallway, but in terms of collaborations I have only participated in someone else's art project because the artist asked me to. I took it very seriously because I was not making much progress with my own work and needed another creative activity to focus on for a bit'. For Nadine, exchanges or collaborations are not about input and output, but about creating a relationship of trust. 'I think the better you understand people from other disciplines, the better you are able to build these links. That is where I see the added value of this place'.

Some people got into the building by way of low-key collaborations. Laetitia de Veth originally made screen prints but moved into an entirely different area of creative practice when she moved to the Volkskrant building. 'I actually wanted to start a screen printing center in the Volkskrant building that could be used by people in and outside of the building', recalls Laetitia.

> But I knew someone who was already part of one of the groups in the building. She told me there were lots of internal struggles, so I thought "sod it, I don't want to be part of that". Then, much later, I was visiting my friend who had started a belly dance studio on the second floor and decided to put a table into her studio for one afternoon each week where I could sit and draw. It was blissfully quiet; a lovely space. Bit by bit I started to ask people from the same floor to volunteer their hands or feet so I could practice making henna tattoos. This is how I got to know everyone on this floor. I somehow felt that once I was in, I would be there for good.

Laetitia quickly got her own studio space and has continued to focus on henna tattoos ever since.

### Hyper-'Grutters'

On the second floor, which housed a mixture of small start-up companies and independent coders, actual business were incubated. These entrepreneurs had initially moved into shared spaces in order to keep their businesses, in typical start-up lingo, 'lean'. Peter Robinett, an American coder who originally moved to Amsterdam to start a magazine on European politics and culture, was the first among them. He gradually brought in others to share his workspace and says that this was initially in order to keep expenses low. 'I used to rely on the tech community in Amsterdam much more than the people in this place', Peter says.

But from 2010, a side-effect occurred. Various techies who initially rented desk space in Peter's office, teamed up and started their own companies. Two such startups, one called Bottlenose and the other Spaaza, moved on to rent their own offices further down the same hallway. Both companies raised impressive amounts of investment and expanded their staff shortly after moving out of Peter's office. 'My office might be the best Amsterdam incubator', Peter wrote on his blog, only half-joking. Being in close proximity to one another allowed this group to quickly ask each other for advice on technical issues. And philosophizing about new technological applications over lunch could lay the foundation for future collaborations. Unsurprisingly, this group would later move into an office space elsewhere in the city in order to maintain their work environment.

Jaap Draaisma had mixed feelings about the commercial creativity that started to populate the Volkskrant building. 'Basically, what those app guys want is to create something and sell it for a lot of money. Obviously I would like to see that whole system of investing and selling collapse. But I do like the entrepreneurial and the nerdy side of it, only I think it can be done differently'. Some of the software developers in the building were connected to Appsterdam, a bottom-up network of app developers, or to Bits of Freedom, a non-profit for online privacy. Jaap Schoufour also noticed the entrance of the commercially creative into Amsterdam's art factories, but in contrast to Jaap Draaisma, he applauds the phenomenon. 'The breeding place policy is about making a city that is as crazy and as diverse as Amsterdam, as dynamic as possible. Where new things are happening all the time, where you can be surprised with the odd mixtures that ended up in a building together. The core of the creative city is that it continues to renew itself', says Jaap Schoufour, indicating that technology startups might as well be part of the mix.

There is an interesting parallel to draw between the group who became known as 'grutters' and turned squats into legal venues which were able to generate income, and the entrepreneurs of startup businesses. Both social groups had an attitude of going against the grain, which was at least partly inspired by the economic crises which formed the backdrop of their activities. Whereas the money flows of the alternative economies of cultural squats cannot be compared to the hyper-capitalist ambitions of the most successful startup companies (in other words, those eventually acquired by Facebook or Google), both groups embrace the insecurities that come with being outside of standard organizational structures. And both groups value the disruptiveness of their own practices, in the sense that even without success, the energy that is generated in the attempt is what makes the endeavor worthwhile. Of course, the big, fat irony of this comparison is that even with the risks for failure being high, the startup movement has made subversive entrepreneurialism - and the aesthetics that come with it - the non-subversive ideal type of neoliberal capitalism, whereas the entrepreuner-squatters initially thought they could get rid of capital altogether.

Their capitalist ambitions aside, the social atmosphere of the second floor techies did generate a weekly event which the larger networks of the building could benefit from: nerd yoga. Started in January 2012, every Wednesday around lunchtime the techies would descend from the second floor into the basement of the Volkskrant building. There, they rented a dance studio (one among three in the entire building) for their weekly yoga practice. The hardest adjustment for them was not practicing between ballet barres and framed pictures of tutus, but the fact that their smartphones had no reception for a full hour. However, they persevered and even attracted other techies working elsewhere in the city to the Volkskrant building in order to join the class. Word spread, so much so that nerd yoga made it to being featured on the internationally-read technology blog Venture Beat.

Esma Linnemann knew none of the nerd yogis but loved the initiative because of its bottom-up character. 'I think it is important that things emerge organically. She may have a point, because when Urban Resort started to organize a monthly drinks reception, it mainly attracted relatively new tenants. The people from the fifth and fourth floors, the tightest and oldest networks of the building, never went because they organized their own get-togethers, mostly at Canvas or at their own studios. The irony of the situation is that once communities emerged within the Volkskrant building, they could and would thrive without Urban Resort. Urban Resort's Merijn Foet expresses this thought when he says: 'I wonder to what extent tenants feel affinity with what we stand for as an organization. Perhaps it is not possible to establish a shared identity that includes both us as an organization, and the community of tenants'.

**Transformers**

If there ever was an instance where the top-down efforts of Urban Resort and tenants' too-cool-for-school attitude of 'letting things happen' merged successfully, it must have been the Transformers Festival. Instigated in 2009, this infrequent festival offered a blend of workshops, late night concerts, organic food and experimental art. Tenants contributed by exhibiting their work, performing, DJing, or designing and did so against a negligible fee. From the early afternoon throughout the entire following night, the Volkskrant building was full of curious neighbors, friends from the former squatting scene, tenants' acquaintances, and random party people. Urban Resort's staff pulled a few all-nighters to make all of this happen, but the end result was one of great fun shared by tenants, organizers and visitors.

Although most tenants were very sympathetic towards 'the landlord's' attempts at organizing parties and festivals, even when they would not necessarily participate themselves, it was the presence of city officials that invoked the skepticism Urban Resort was trying to avoid. Marjolein van der Wal, a fashion designer and performance artist whose studio was packed with rhinestones and alien costumes: 'When I participated in the 2012 edition of the Transformers Festival, I think most of the visitors in the afternoon came from the city government. We organized this art market, and all I could think was: where are all the hipster girls that should be here? It wasn't exactly attracting the right audience'. On the other hand, the festival also attracted festival organizers looking to scout new talent. Jesse Limmen for instance, put his Magneetbar ['magnetic bar'] at the festival and was spotted by the organizers of Lowlands, the largest pop festival of the Netherlands. His bar being part of Lowlands for five years eventually led to his own festival, Magneetfestival, on the eastern outskirts of Amsterdam.

When the Volkskrant building art factory reached its sixth anniversary, it had become difficult to pinpoint which of the Volkskrant building's 'successes' were the result of Urban Resort's efforts, and which of these were entirely 'bottom-up'. Canvas would have gone bankrupt without Urban Resort's leniency towards paying rent, and would not have been able to act as a platform for the many DJ's from the building. The graphic designers, performance artists and music producers from the creative community on the fifth floor would have had more difficulties in achieving their artistic goals if rents would have been higher. And finally, the start-up community could grow stronger and larger not only due to their own hard work but also because of Urban Resort's flexibility in facilitating them.

The building on the night of its opening as the Volkshotel.

# Chapter 4

# ENTER THE VOLKSHOTEL – 2013 AND ONWARDS

If the previous chapters have shown us anything, it is that the building's buzz was an odd combination of a bit of good old squatting spirit with the otherwise smoothly managed construction of Amsterdam's creative city machine. During the kick-off phase this worked extremely well, imbuing the building with a feeling of real and unlimited possibility. As the building matured, it became increasingly clear that an art factory and a squat are rather different concepts. Having to follow rules and regulations as well as having to pay rent turned out to be game changers for our band of ex-squatters. Nonetheless, the building became a lively hub for creatives of all stripes - not least of all due to the serendipitous processes Urban Resort made space for, of which a substantial part were also related to Canvas. Although the venue's success was not achieved overnight, once put on the map, it became a place to be not only for Volkskrant tenants, artistic folk, and the occasional city planning official.

> 'I cycled past the Volkskrant building, which I knew only from going to Canvas, and suddenly thought "this could be the ideal building"'.

All sorts of people began to make their way to the top floor of the Volkskrant building. One of them was Job Heimans, an entrepreneur similar to those on the second floor of the building described in the previous chapter. He had sold his startup enterprise to the big software company Oracle, and was now looking for an investment to use the money he had made. From 2008 onwards, Job went to Canvas every now and then for a drink, but it was only in October 2010 that he suddenly looked at the place with different eyes. 'I was on the lookout for a building to start a hotel in. I wanted the rooms to be quite cheap, so it had to be outside of the city center. I cycled past the Volkskrant building, which I knew only from going to Canvas, and suddenly thought "this could be the ideal building"'.

Job's inspiration for the type of hotel that he wanted to start came from a hotel in Berlin called Michelberger. He had visited it for the first time in July of that same year and had made it a habit to stay there whenever he visited the German capital, which was every two weeks at that time. 'Every time I was there I thought how much fun it would be if I could do something like that myself. It was different than all the other hotels I had stayed at, it surprised me. I like any hotel that has a decent coffee bar, but this one also changed into a great spot to have a beer or cocktail at night. The staff were the type of people that could have been your friends'. He decided to start a similar hotel in Amsterdam and the Volkskrant building triggered his curiosity. On the first of December 2010, Job sent a letter to the housing corporation still owning the building, which had changed its name from Het Oosten to Stadgenoot, inquiring whether the building was for sale. A few weeks later Stadgenoot called him and said that it indeed was.

**Big Money**

As it happened, Urban Resort was also in the market to buy. Since the beginning of the Volkskrant building project, it had been their goal to purchase property. Having assets would allow them to consolidate their position and expand their organization. So when the housing corporation Stadgenoot put the building on the market, Urban Resort wanted to try and buy it. Not having any substantial capital, they had to find an investor first. Some years before, one of Urban Resort's initiators, Fred Stammeshaus, had convinced his old friend and former alderman Duco Stadig to become chair of Urban Resort. This gave the old squatters a strategically more advantageous position towards, not only the authorities, but investors as well. Duco: 'I knew an investor who was willing to make an offer on the building. He would let Urban Resort continue with the art factory for another ten years. After that he would be free to do with it as he pleased and by that time the area would have picked up even more'.

. . . . . . . . .



. . . . . . . . .

All of a sudden the old squatters were rubbing shoulders with property investors. While their relationship with the city council had become a stable one, dealing with old money was definitely a challenge and a cause for serious headaches. Nevertheless, the opportunity of running the art factory for another ten years seemed too good to pass. So they teamed up and put in an offer, which turned out to be not high enough. Job Heimans' offer eventually was accepted and he became the new owner of the building. 'That was a crushing blow', says Duco. This new situation meant that Urban Resort was either out or needed to somehow find a way to collaborate with him. That is, if he was interested in such a collaboration at all.

Perhaps surprisingly, he was. He figured that independent art studios and small creative companies could fit well into his concept of an informal, hip and artsy hotel, and therefore did not think of getting rid of the art factory at all, so he says. But Duco Stadig is somewhat skeptical as

to the entrepreneur's self-declared instant enthusiasm for the arty semi-squat. 'He had no other choice but to keep at least part of the art factory, because the borough would not give him a
license just to build yet another hotel. They would not do that, because we had convinced them
not to do so, with the help of the city. That is how such a process works'. Jaap Draaisma adds
that Urban Resort was not the underdog in this process. 'It was really because of our great
network in local government that we were able to partly keep the building for non-profit ends'.

When Job contacted Urban Resort to talk about collaborating, Jaap Draaisma had mixed feelings. 'When Job wanted to work together with us, my first reaction was, let's say, skeptical. I
think it is ridiculous to pay such a high price for a building, or to even have that kind of money'.
But Jaap was not the only one having mixed feelings. Job himself had visited the art factory
on his own in order to get a feel for the place and was rather disappointed. 'I sneaked into
the building around three times, just to see what was going on', Job says. 'I would just enter
through whichever door was left open. Let's say that I found that the marketing of the place
was better than the reality. Everything looked a bit worn out, and lots of doors were closed'.
His observation nicely illustrates the difference between discourse and reality when it comes to
urban creative spaces. With the slick images of creative showcase projects in mind, encoun-
tering the reality of a run down building where people simply do their (art)work can feel quite
disappointing.

Job's initial interest in the building really was due to Canvas. In building his business case for
the hotel, he quickly had Thijs Timmers on board. Job would invest in Canvas' renovation and
expansion, and of course the hotel would attract new visitors to the nightclub. Furthermore,
Canvas would acquire a permanent status, getting rid of the precarity the endeavor had had
from the beginning. So initially, it looks as if Job Heimans was simply interested in setting up a
Michelberger-like hotel, and wanted to build on Canvas' image and success. The size and location of the Volkskrant building fit the bill as well. Keeping the art factory might not have been
on Job's mind right from the start, but he somehow came around on that too.



The idea of a collaboration started to grow on both Urban Resort and Job Heimans. Jaap
Draaisma:

> Step by step, Job warmed to the idea that the art factory had to be part of his plan. He had
> been talking to other parties as well, but he had realized that they would turn the place into
> something else. So he was serious about working with us. He did not want to use us as an
> instrument, or an alibi, but really wanted to create workspaces, just like we had done. His

respect for what we have achieved with the Volkskrant building was genuine. This meant we had the confidence to put our conditions on the table. We thought: "if you want us to continue with what we have done with the Volkskrant building, it has to be our way".

The relationship between Urban Resort and Job Heimans became more intense again when Cor van Zadelhoff, a founder of DTZ, one of Europe's biggest property brokers, entered into the picture. He had co-invested in the Volkskrant building with Job Heimans and the two had decided they wanted to start renovating the building in 2013 instead of in 2014. But almost all two hundred tenants of the Volkskrant building had rental contracts until 2014. It would be tricky to get them to leave earlier, and they would certainly need the help of Urban Resort to achieve this.

· · · · · · · ·

'It was bizarre that after being involved in this diplomatic attempt to
nip the law in the bud, I now had to look at
Van Zadelhoff as a potential business partner'.

· · · · · · · ·

Although squatters have never been fond of property investors, Cor van Zadelhoff was a particularly bitter pill to swallow for the Urban Resort people. Some of them were old enemies from the time when Van Zadelhoff funded the political campaigns against squatting. The right-wing parties eventually proposed an anti-squatting law which was accepted in 2010. Prior to that, in 2009, Dutch Labor Party minister Ellen Vogelaar had organized an informal meeting at Canvas with the help of Urban Resort and representatives of the squatting movement, to come up with a protest against the proposed law against squatting. Many politicians were present and the event had to be kept secret. 'It was bizarre that after being involved in this diplomatic attempt to nip the law in the bud, I now had to look at Van Zadelhoff as a potential business partner', Jaap Draaisma says.

But for the sake of keeping at least a part of the building, the former squatters accepted his involvement and decided they were willing to help Job Heimans in getting his hotel to open earlier, but on a strict condition. They wanted to be able to continue doing things their way, even if they were to manage the smaller art factory. 'After all, we had to empty the building extremely fast, convince tenants to leave, make expenses', explains Jaap Draaisma. 'We had to make sure that two hundred legal tenants would give up their contracts one year early', he adds. He and Duco agreed with Job that if they managed to get enough tenants out by July 2013, Urban Resort would be hired by Job to manage the new and smaller art factory. They could do so according to their own vision and principles of low rent, collectivism, and self-management.

This meant they were neither responsible to the owner of the building anymore, nor to their tenants as a landlord, leaving them in the extraordinary position to focus on the things they always deemed most important about art factories: the atmosphere, the experiment of it, and the people. Duco:

What Urban Resort had now was a place that was not theirs, not even theirs to rent. But they do get to decide who gets a studio space there, define what type of place it becomes, organize things their way. And Job gets to show off with a fun and authentic place next to the hotel. He also hopes, and we will see if that is the case, that people from the art factory will do things that are of interest to the hotel guests.

Although the smaller art factory in the back will adhere to all standards set by the Art Factory Bureau, it no longer receives funding from the city government.

**Sounds of Protest**
So Urban Resort had agreed to help the adventurous entrepreneur and his right-wing investor in getting tenants to give up their workspaces earlier. But what did the tenants themselves think? At the beginning of October 2012, Job Heimans and Bas van de Geyn from Urban Resort investigated, among all tenants, whether they were willing to vacate earlier. They did so by arranging meetings with groups of tenants from different floors. At these meetings, Job presented his plans and explained that he needed tenants' co-operation in order to be able to open his Volkshotel in spring 2014.

· · · · · · · ·

Although the smaller art factory in the back will adhere to all standards set by the Art Factory Bureau, it no longer receives funding from the city government.

· · · · · · · ·

During these meetings, many tenants expressed their enthusiasm for the multi-functional building comprising hotel, club, restaurant, co-working space, meeting rooms, and renovated workspaces. Heimans' plans of bringing artwork by tenants into the hotel's foyer, or having touring bands record something in one of the music studios in the basement, were met with approval. The promise of free access to the planned hot tubs on the rooftop might have had something to do with that, too. Following these meetings, all tenants were asked to choose between three options. The first was leaving the building before July 1st of 2013 in exchange for a financial compensation, the second was cooperating with Job's plan in order to get a new studio in the renewed part of the building, and the third was staying until 2014. The only problematic choice was the third, because if all tenants would opt for that, it would obstruct earlier construction of the hotel. Job said an early transition would happen if the percentage of tenants unwilling to cooperate with his plan was below ten percent.

The positive reactions during these meetings were not entirely representative of what many people in the building felt. Shortly after Job had made his plans known, a group of tenants from the second floor got together and wrote a letter in which they stated they would stay as long as their rental contract allowed them to, and would not cooperate with an earlier transition. This group consisted of a mixture of internet entrepreneurs and artists. However, this conspiracy quickly dispersed due to lack of shared interests.

Some individual tenants were unhappy with the plans and decided to leave instead of protesting. The Serbian sound engineer Slobodan Bajic, who moved to the Netherlands in 1993 to go to art school, was one of them. 'Job Heimans wants to make this into a hip and slick place. He is not really concerned with culture, only with the hip image culture has', Slobodan says. Urban Resort's old friend Julien Haffmans, who had remained a tenant of the Volkskrant building up until this point, was another one. She was not happy with the way in which Job Heimans phrased his plans to the tenants. Julien:

> By bringing the values of capitalism into the building he unwittingly damages the thing he buys. There is a mean paradox at work when a party wants to preserve and exploit a culture or community by buying its housing. Job continuously talks about the investment he made into the building and how happy tenants should be with that, and tenants start to adopt that logic. They miss the underlying problem: Who created the value Job bought? And whom did he pay to acquire that value? By bringing the values of capitalism into the Volkskrant-community he unwittingly damages the culture he bought into.

But the only two real instances of organized protest against Job's plan came from the fourth and the sixth floor. The fourth floor consisted mainly of artists who were very pleased with the relaxed atmosphere on their floor and valued each other's expertise. They were afraid to lose their inspiring environment if the renewed and smaller art factory would not have room for all of them. So instead of showing up on the assigned time slot, according to the schedule Job Heimans had given them, they insisted on speaking to him as a group. Theater set designer Marouscha Levy felt their experience with working in such a place, and thereby shaping it, was not being recognized: 'Job wants to create a Berlin-like place. Well, I work there a lot and you cannot compare the two cities. In Berlin, rents are much lower, there is more space available. Their plan might work for people who work on laptops, but we need space. It feels as if that which has been made by us is now being used by them'.

Although eager to keep their group together, the fourth floor artists did not manage to continue to speak with one voice. Eventually, many tenants of this group strategically signed for co-operation because they figured that if everyone said they wanted to stay, no smaller art factory could be created anyway. The other trouble Job had was with a group of independent filmmakers and editors from the sixth floor. They had moved to the Volkskrant building together from another art factory and were joined later by a duo of a photographer and a film editor. The group quickly connected to other tenants on the same floor, among whom was illustrator Mirthe Blussé. 'I exactly remember the day they moved here. I met them and it just felt right, I think we share the same values', says Mirthe. The filmmakers were used to working together and got a large space which they divided into different sections. 'We invested quite some time and money in our place, because it is important that it reflects who you are as an artist', says filmmaker Daan Veldhuizen.

The filmmakers and other creative entrepreneurs from the sixth floor had decided to act as a group in negotiating with Job Heimans from the start. A factor in this was that they discovered they had been exposed to asbestos in their workspaces. This had put them on their guard for other disappointments from the side of those in charge of the building they worked at. In their meeting with Job Heimans, they stressed the importance of collective effort in making an art factory of value. 'If you want to sustain the creative character of this building, you have to acknowledge that it has emerged organically, and that you will now disrupt that', Daan said. When Job mentioned they could have a lower rent if they would take up certain chores for the sake of the art factory, this was met with much protest. 'If those things don't happen spontaneously, it won't work at all', Mirthe said. 'When we organize a documentary night we don't do that for bloody tourists. It has to be ours. You make it sound as if we are puppets in your show, while we have actually created it', Daan added. This group managed to negotiate having work spaces in the new art factory close to one another and were also given additional possibilities for financial compensation during construction. The latter applied to everyone in the building. Once everyone had moved studios in the building and Job Heimans' company had officially started commissioning Urban Resort to run the art factory on his behalf, Daan would eventually become the spokesperson for the art factory community.

It would take until the first of November 2012 before Job Heimans would decide he would go ahead with earlier construction works. 'I completely underestimated the amount of work that went into talking to all tenants', he admits. He thinks this is due to the type of people that work in the Volkskrant building. 'If you ask a question to an economically oriented company, you can expect a clear "yes" or "no". With creative people, the answer to my question remained very vague for a long time'.

· · · · · · · ·

'If you ask a question to an economically oriented company, you can expect a clear "yes" or "no". With creative people, the answer to my question remained very vague for a long time'.

· · · · · · · ·

After a tense and busy period of negotiations with tenants, organized by Urban Resort's Bas van de Geyn, the overall reactions from tenants were surprisingly positive. Many tenants hoped that the more professional coolness that would come with Volkshotel would extend to their businesses. Some saw business opportunities straight away, for instance in designing for the interior of the hotel. Ironically, while Urban Resort had always intended to create a place away from the commercial realm, many tenants seemed more than happy to become part of such a commercial endeavor. And as it turned out, the hotel's management would later go on to commission certain art factory residents to design the interior of some of the more exclusive rooms of the Volkshotel.

## Moving Out

So in November 2012, Job and Urban Resort decided that tenants who had agreed to leave would have to do so before the first of July 2013. The process of leaving went remarkably well, says Jaap Draaisma. 'We could offer people money to leave, and with the help of other organizations they could find new workspaces. Actually it went super-smoothly', says Jaap. As soon as the tenants had left, the basement was renovated in order to accommodate more advanced sound studios. On the second floor, the plaster walls that had been constructed by enthusiastic, but unprofessional, tenants were replaced with proper walls. The renewed art factory now only comprised the basement and back wing of the ground floor, first floor and second floor. By the time July was nearing, the hallways of the building were full of furniture that had been left behind by tenants. Urban Resort had urged everyone to take along what was theirs, but it may well be that some of it had belonged to *De Volkskrant*. Starting July 2013, the Volkskrant building almost hosted more construction workers than creative professionals.

The tenants who had decided to stay had to move as well, from one studio to another. Some even had to move several times within the building. On the one hand, they were full of anticipation about the new Volkshotel they would become part of. Many felt it was a step forward and thought the renewed Volkskrant building would mean something for their own professionalism too. Jakob, for instance, regularly DJs at Canvas and therefore welcomed the attempt of making the club more mature. 'Amsterdam needs a serious place with an international image, with a decent club', he said in support of Job's plans. On the other hand, the construction work was causing tenants a lot of trouble. Many felt they were entitled to paying less rent and said so to Job in September 2013. He declined their request but did offer a budget to each floor in order to decorate the hallways or buy furniture for the few communal areas. Curator Viola van Alphen responded: 'It is a nice gesture but really, we want the hallways to look nice as well. So don't worry about that, Job'.

This raises the old question of who is responsible for such a site of creative production: the collective or the manager? Job, Urban Resort and the remaining tenants were struggling with the same issues as Kaos and Urban Resort were at the beginning of their project: how much freedom should there be? When do you let things happen, and when do you actively manage them? In 2007, the spaces for creative production catered to the artists using them, with the intention that these places were opened up to the neighborhood from time to time. By 2014, the spaces of creative production had gone from this somewhat nebulous social function, to an economic function: they now had to contribute to the arty image of the Volkshotel, and would therefore indirectly help to generate revenue. Some tenants were very much aware of this element. 'After the hotel opens, us artists should actually be paid if we hang out at Canvas', Marouscha Levy said only half-jokingly.

Of course, the ways in which the Volkshotel will become successful (or not), will be very different from what the successes (and the failures) of the art factory looked like. What we have been trying to do so far is to look at the six years in which the Volkskrant building was an art factory only. First of all, situating it against the Amsterdam-specific context of a rich subcultural scene, fueled by squatting practices but also certainly by the eventual approval of the city's politicians. Secondly, we have delved into the events that marked the early years of the art factory, showing how challenging financial circumstances went hand in hand with great excitement and truly inspiring parties, initiatives, and other projects. Finally, we have shown which key elements led to the art factory becoming what it became: of interest to commercial entrepreneurs who see the potential of the creative scene in attracting visitors to a hotel. In spite of the stark contrast this forms with the origins of the art factory, it was also an opportunity for both the tenants and Urban Resort to make the place they had created together more financially healthy and sustainable. The question, of course, is: will it also remain healthy and sustainable in terms of its creativity and its subversive practices? Will the musicians still be smoking marijuana in the hallways? Will an artist in-between residencies still feel free enough to sleep in her studio for a short time? Only time will tell.

## The Volkshotel and Its Legacy

At the official opening of the Volkshotel on June 27, 2014, Urban Resort and Cor van Zadelhoff shared the stage. Jaap Draaisma decided not to let the odd match go unnoticed for the large audience, and stated in his speech that he wanted to see the Volkshotel as a continuation of the alternative, affordable spaces of Amsterdam. Making references to Urban Resort's roots, he placed the new creative hotel in a lineage that began with Provo, much to the amused disapproval of Van Zadelhoff. 'I was pleased to be able to take a position, there and then, without attempting to make a compromise. Van Zadelhoff and us, we are very much aware of our opposite positions, yet we could share in the achievement of the Volkshotel'.

Apart from the smaller art factory in the back wing and the hotel, for which some tenants designed the interior of a few special rooms, the Volkshotel also has a co-working area and café on the ground floor. To celebrate the opening of this heavily stylized space full of vintage décor and a piano, a special beer was brewed by Oedipus, a trendy micro-brewery renting space in another one of Urban Resort's buildings. Frank Sheppard, a once famous American actor who has been part of Amsterdam's alternative scene for decades, provided some musical entertainment. Incidentally, he was also one of the first to perform at Canvas when it was just starting out in 2007. This organic pulling together of loosely connected actors and scenes is what the Volkskrant building eventually did best. Staying rooted in an activist background while listening to the heartbeat of the ever renewing creative scene became its most defining feature. With the aim of generating a very steep return on investment, it seems clear that the character of the Volkshotel will be rather different from the old Volkskrant building. Let's hope this difference is going to be an interesting one.

The sign of night club Trouw through the window of an empty studio as tenants were moving out.

# Chapter 5

# CONCLUSION: FAILING FORWARD

In this concluding chapter, we will assess the art factory project from the point of view of the different stakeholders and try to locate the Volkskrant building experiment within the wider processes of social transformation we are currently experiencing. We will do so starting with the viewpoint of the tenants, moving on to the viewpoint of the city, and finishing with the viewpoint of Urban Resort. This will lead us to the notion of performative defiance as a way of understanding the trajectory the Volkskrant building has taken with regard to the initial ideological ambitions of the ex-squatters of Urban Resort. Performative defiance, we argue, describes the mode of engagement with the political and economic realities that, more or less consciously, accepts the likelihood of its own failure, yet understands it in terms of failing forward. This is to say that while working towards a likely point at which the project is co-opted by forces one cannot control anymore (and probably doesn't agree with) it is the process itself that generates practices making the eventual failure worthwhile.

It is the logic of such generative processes and the alternative social practices they engender that will then form the subject of the second part of this conclusion. We are going to take a step back from the clamor of activities around the Volkskrant building per se and try to take the short history of the art factory as our point of departure for a reflection on the value of 'alternative' infrastructures as a breeding ground for timely and participative forms of citizenship, especially in light of the disciplined modes of moving through urban space we are currently faced with.

## The Tenants

From the beginning, nobody expected the process of transforming the old Volkskrant building into an art factory to be smooth sailing. Yet, in spite of the challenges the project encountered along the way, it is fair to say that for most of the Volkskrant building's tenants, it was indeed a success. Most obviously, it was successful in terms of providing a new generation of workspace to a new generation of artistic and creative producers. Thanks to the Volkskrant building, they had access to affordable studios and offices from where many a career was successfully launched. And while the initial fantasy of an infinitely expanding building made way for real growth pain and ideological disillusionment, the building remained a special place, something different from the mainstream.

What our study of the Volkskrant building shows, as well, is that the idea of 'synergies' spontaneously arising when creative producers are put in physical proximity is a slightly more complicated affair than the creative city nomenclature tends to believe. In our own experience as researchers of creative hubs, flex-working operations, and co-working spaces, it is clear that the much-vaunted synergies are a fairly rare occasion in most settings and certainly nothing that crops up automatically. Research shows that if one wants synergies to arise, they need to be facilitated and even then, they are hardly a structural occurrence.[39] At the Volkskrant building, the idea that tenants could interact with each other across floors was constrained by the fact that they were allowed permission to their own floors only. This meant interaction became incidental: at parties or receptions, or on Canvas' terrace during an after work beer, but not when you needed each other for work. This, it seems to us, tends to be the situation in many creative hubs and buildings hosting different (creative) entrepreneurs. There will always be some kind of stratification or division simply because people are there to get their work done.

Hence, we believe that the lesson here is to get rid of the idea that spaces for creative entrepreneurs should, above all, feature the systematic creation of synergies. Positive contingencies and valuable encounters should, and will be, a great side effect, yet there should be other, more realistic motivations and objectives guiding the setup of a creative hub. A possible alternative starting point could be found in the provision of work space that is affordable for autonomous (art) practitioners, as well as a way to open up the functionality of creativity as business towards creative disruption understood strictly in the artistic and non-Californian sense of the term.[40]

* * * * * * * *

Positive contingencies and valuable encounters should, and will be, a great side effect, yet there should be other, more realistic motivations and objectives guiding the setup of a creative hub.

* * * * * * * *

We also find that sometimes these spaces turn into scenes for experimentation with new types of solidarity among creative workers; a much-needed thing in a time of increasingly flexible labor conditions, especially in the creative industries.[41] One example of this is the setting up of a Bread Fund (collective disability insurance) among self-employed creative workers, which has in fact just been initiated by one of the Volkskrant building's tenants. Again, time will have to tell whether such practices have the capacity to contribute to a city's creative scene in a significant way, but for now it is important to note that such 'uncreative' collaborations should not be overlooked. They have at least the potential to bring about collective practices acting as an antidote against the individualizing tendencies of neoliberal work conditions.

**The City**

There is no doubt that the Volkskrant building as art factory did a great service to the city of Amsterdam. And this is not only reflected by the high sales price Job Heimans had to pay for it when taking over the building. Sure, for the city's accountants and policy makers, turning a profit in an otherwise very difficult property market proved that their pioneering strategy of alternative creative city development worked. The physical state of the building alone does not explain its worth of seven million euros, but its location on the cultural map of the city, and beyond, does. What has certainly helped, as well, is the rise of other cultural and trendy venues in the immediate area, such as the renowned techno club Trouw across the street, and the various independently-owned boutiques and cafes in walking distance from the Volkskrant building. The fact that Canvas became a preferred spot for hip city dwellers and visitors has certainly rubbed off onto the rest of the area.



However, more important than the financial value creation, is the Volkskrant building's contribution to the cultural life of the city. Regardless of all the problems that occur when idealism is confronted with the everyday realities of running a building and the necessity of increasing the rent, Urban Resort has always offered room to different subcultural scenes. Events that are now firmly established on the subcultural map of Amsterdam, such as the Burning Man-inspired Magneetfestival, theatre festival De Parade, and hip hop event Appelsap, have had their headquarters at the Volkskrant building at some point.

Going back to the beginning stages in 2007, we can recall Hessel Dokkum's statement that it was a mistake to choose the Volkskrant building for Urban Resort's first project. Looking at the initial ambitions for the building then, we must conclude that some of them could not be achieved to the extent that was initially hoped for. One of them was the effect the Volkskrant building was intended to have on its immediate neighborhood. Apart from attracting guests to Canvas and to the Transformers Festival, the art factory did not, in the long run, manage to involve the surrounding neighborhood through exhibitions, workshops, and other planned activities. This is an interesting finding in light of the policy ambitions connected to these kinds of projects. While the facilitation of internal synergies - as we have seen above - already presents a formidable challenge, this is even more so with regard to external ones. The expectations of 'uplifting' effects of art factories on the social situation of the local population are a staple fantasy of creative city planners, policy makers, and experts with regard to projects like the Volkskrant building, but in reality these effects hardly ever register. As we have indicated above, there is a certain 'place making effect' in the sense of gentrification and hipster culture, yet the more holistic claim of 'improving the neighborhood' cannot be substantiated.

This should not be surprising at all: unless they are forced by contract to engage in social activities - say, in exchange for financial concessions - creative producers are going to focus on their immediate professional activities. Not because they are anti-social, but simply because they already have enough on their plates.

**Urban Resort's Practices**

The practices of Urban Resort can be seen as a practical critique of neoliberal capitalism, one that criticizes the existing system by engaging with it - as a process of constantly searching for space in order to construct 'different worlds'.[42] As we have seen, the founding members of Urban Resort received their fair share of critique from the more radical quarters of the activist and squatters community they still consider themselves part of. 'We continue to fight for the autonomy of our places, but the question is how we put our ideology into practice', says Jaap Draaisma. 'Sometimes people accuse me of being too commercial. But in the end it is about seizing opportunities while staying true to your principles'. The decision to pragmatically engage with the forces of the state and the market, is seen by many of the former comrades as something close to an act of treason. And it is true, many of the more radical aspirations of Urban Resort in regard to building self-organizing communities and establishing an alternative economy, could be considered failures. Self-management, as it is understood in squatter terms, never really took off at the Volkskrant building. Although many tenants showed great involvement with the building when they were afraid to lose their workspaces, the actual management of the building has remained in the hands of Urban Resort, creating a customer relationship with their tenants against their own will.

However, we need to take a closer look here. Although some of the plans for the Volkskrant building have failed, we have seen that it has been a case of failing forward. In fact, it seems to us that failing forward represents the limit of achievement for this kind of practical engagement with a system whose rules and values one is essentially opposed to. This is to say that given the conflicting sets of values between a relatively weak actor such as Urban Resort and 'the system' (the city administration, the market, etc.), it should be clear that in the long run, success will be determined by the logic of the powers that be. Thus, in a way, outright success was never really in the cards for Urban Resort. Failing forward, could then be described as a mode of activism defined by the ethos of performative defiance: rather than 'resisting' the power of the state and the market, one engages with them in order to find out practically where new openings and spaces for alternative social practices are. This kind of strategy always involves dimensions of complicity, as well as the real danger of dressing up policies one is ideologically opposed to.



However, even with the new situation of running an art factory subsidized by a commercial business (rather than the city), new spaces for alternative practices might open up; new strategies and alliances could be experimented with. Formally speaking, Urban Resort can now focus on the social aspect, or the cultural content, of the place they run. Where they previously struggled with the building's many practical problems, they now do not have to worry about those things anymore. Yet, this begs the question: what exactly will they do then? What are they capable of? If there is suddenly room for more than just renting out rooms, they will have to show what they got.

## Performative Defiance

The advantage of Urban Resort's strategy of performative defiance is that they actually have the opportunity to find out. Even if the Volkshotel turns out to be a dead end for Urban Resort, they at least have tried this unlikely kind of alliance. In our assessment, the willingness to test the waters of neoliberal city making for openings in which the new practices of autonomy and difference can emerge and find new modes of existence, is absolutely crucial.[43] It is here that we see real social innovation at work, that is, in the interstices of the market and creative city policies, where the practical resistance against the neoliberal and technocratic tendencies of social standardization survives. The importance of these experiments in failing forward lies in their defiance of policy makers, city planners, and experts who always already know what the best infrastructures are 'for the people'. This is social innovation as a form of active, participatory citizenship that today, it seems to us, will always have to have a strong hold in an ethos of performative defiance as well.

· · · · · · · ·

Failing forward, could then be described as a mode of activism
defined by the ethos of performative defiance.

· · · · · · · ·

In continuing to fail forward, Urban Resort makes a crucial contribution to the contemporary struggle for our cities. The defiance they, as well as other initiatives and projects, show - in Amsterdam these would include collectives such as OT301, Schijnheilig, De Valreep and a number of others - point to a possible future of urban politics as citizen's craft. The emergence of defiant citizenship depends on the existence of such spaces. Our societies need infrastructures where 'alternative' - for lack of a better term - social practices can be experienced and experimented with. This is even more important as we stand on the eve of an enormous roll-out of smart city technology and digital agendas that threaten us city dwellers with an unprecedented level of social control.

In such a situation, the question of urban infrastructure has become one of absolute political and social urgency.[44] There certainly is no lack of fashionable ideas as to the nature of the kind of infrastructures we need in order to deal with the challenges we are facing as societies. Not a day passes in which big technology corporations and policy makers do not advertise their solutions for a better future. We have already mentioned smart city technologies, but also sharing, social innovation, sustainability, and resilience are some of the buzzwords that function as disguises for the disempowerment of the urban citizenry.[45] In this context, we think it worthwhile to take a step back for a moment and reflect on the changing relationship between citizenship and infrastructure. This is what we are going to do for the remainder of this concluding chapter.

## Citizenship and Social Infrastructure

The discipline of sociology has shown, since its very beginnings, that for a society to function, what is needed is an infrastructure in which forms of active citizenship can be invented and transmitted. If one wanted to put this negatively, one could say that a network of social institutions is required that disciplines and formats the multitude of human beings into a civilized, homogeneous people. This indeed runs as a central theme through the modern thinking about society. What comes to mind is Emile Durkheim's work on religion,[46] Max Weber's focus on bureaucracy,[47] or Norbert Elias' theory of the civilizing process,[48] to name only a few canonical contributions. It was of course the French philosopher Michel Foucault who provided the most pointed and provocative formulation of this thesis when he described modern society in terms of an archipelago of institutional 'molds' modeled on Jeremy Bentham's panoptic prison-structure.[49] School, university, factory, office, hospital, union, church, etc.: these panoptic institutions functioned as production sites for disciplined citizens. According to Foucault, their synergetic effect was what he called discipline: the generation of human beings conforming to the social, political, economic, and cultural standards of modern mass society and democracy. Social life was disciplined by assigning each citizen his or her position within a panoptic society, thus fixing his or her identity within social space.

As Foucault shows, the emergence of liberal-democratic citizenship was enabled by the application of a particular set of social technologies producing the subjects that were then able to function as modern citizens. Thus, Foucault's writing on discipline revealed the intimate relationship between social structure and citizenship that should be characterized in terms of co-evolution: rather than naively understanding our liberal-democratic order as the apex of political evolution, in the sense of reaching an order that finally suits the natural needs of human beings, what Foucault shows is that human beings are man-made, or rather, institutionally formed.

What needs to be pointed out immediately is that thinking about the relationship between infrastructure and social life does not necessarily have to lead to nightmarish visions of a society modeled upon a particular prison structure. German philosopher Peter Sloterdijk has recently done exactly this. His *Du musst Dein Leben ändern* approaches the question of discipline in terms of the Greek notion of áskesis, the original meaning of which is 'exercise' or 'training'.[50] Sloterdijk fundamentally builds on Foucault's excavation of the relation of social structures/ citizenship but rejects its reduction to a 'dark', manipulative, and somewhat illegitimate force. Rather, he argues, discipline as asceticism should be understood as a dialectical process of self-formation in relation to the formative structure (the molds) of a given society. As Sloterdijk puts it:

> Rather than the prisons and places of repressive surveillance, it is the strict schools and universities as well as the craftsmen's workshops and the artistic studios that provide modernity with the space for the essential "human orthopedics", i.e., the formation of the young according to the standards of Christian-humanist discipline. The actual destination of the

journey into the age of the arts and techniques is the active development of ever new generations of virtuosi.[51]

The 'virtuosi' who Sloterdijk understands as the products of such orthopedics, are human beings able to lead their lives autonomously precisely because they have gone through the formative process of asceticism. What he thus articulates is that institutionalized pedagogic formation is an inherently ambivalent process. It is at once restrictive and the precondition for creative self-transcendence: it does not only force the becoming subject into a 'mold' but in the process of molding, it also transmits the necessary equipment for emancipation by self-modulation.

## Craftsmanship

What we can learn from both Sloterdijk and Foucault is that a meaningful practice of citizenship is predicated on a functioning network of social institutions providing the faculties necessary for the self-formation of political subjectivity. Regardless of whether one understands these processes in terms of repressive discipline or emancipative asceticism, it is impossible to think about citizenship without at once referring to its practical training ground that lies outside the classical sphere of politics.

· · · · · · · · ·

*A meaningful practice of citizenship is predicated on a functioning network of social institutions providing the faculties necessary for the self-formation of political subjectivity.*

· · · · · · · · ·

Richard Sennett's recent intervention on craftsmanship points exactly at this problem. In the classical liberal understanding, craftsmanship has nothing to do with politics. The craftsman is the bourgeois, the economic citizen, and as such qualitatively different from the citoyen [political citizen]. Sennett challenges this dichotomy by arguing that craftsmanship is an institutional practice connecting the worlds of bourgeois and citoyen. As he demonstrates, craftsmanship as the result of a process of dedicated apprenticeship provided a crucial training ground for faculties that are indispensable for a meaningful practice of citizenship.[52] The virtuosity of the craftsman, i.e., the purposeful application of ones body to the shaping of objects, Sennett understands as the precondition for the virtuosity of the citizen in shaping social relations to his fellow citizens. The experience of making a unique contribution through one's engagement with matter, generates the self-consciousness necessary for a meaningful participation in society.

However, Sennett's motivation for writing a book on craftsmanship lies in his conviction that the rapid devaluation of craftsmanship over the last few decades signals the destruction of the continuum of virtuosity. The main source of this destruction Sennett identifies in neoliberal ideology and practice: flexibilization of work, generalized outsourcing, managerialism, and so on, are developments that systematically reduce the experience of making a unique contribution. The continuing reengineering of business processes according to IT-systems, redrafting of organizations of all kinds according to managerial protocols, reorganization of education systems according to 'market requirements', etc., lead to an increasing distance between the bodily experience of work and its eventual outcome (product/service). As the feeling of responsibility toward one's work (what Sennett calls 'the relation with the object') disappears, the continuum of virtuosity breaks down.

The merit of Sennett's argument lies in having made explicit the connection between labor and politics in terms of a continuum of virtuosity. For him, the current political crisis is the result of the failure of one of the crucial institutions of discipline; craftsmanship. The main problem of Sennett's argument is that it is too romantic, yearning for forms of discipline and asceticism that the new generation rejects.[53] And along with it, they reject the old 'training facilities', i.e., the respective institutions, simply because they are not useful to them. The virtuosity that is necessary to navigate today's economic, as well as political, terrain is one totally different from the one Sennett has in mind. It is neither the virtuosity of a bygone era of crafting, nor is it the virtuosity of the factory and the big office - if such a thing ever existed. It is a new kind of virtuosity and this has implications for the contemporary practice of citizenship.

### Virtuosity

The Italian philosopher Paolo Virno recognizes this clearly when he refers to the emergence of a new and very different kind of virtuosity that he links to the immaterialization of the sphere of production.[54] Immaterialization refers to a process by which the immaterial dimension of products, i.e. their symbolic, aesthetic, and social value has come to outweigh their classical material dimension. Images, knowledge, information, codes, affects, as well as social relationships per se have become the predominant factors in determining the value a particular commodity has on the market. In other words, for Virno - who is affiliated with the post-Marxist Italian left - immaterialization stands for what policy makers and mainstream economists refer to in terms of digitization and creative economy.

· · · · · · · ·

The current political crisis is the result of the failure of one of the
crucial institutions of discipline; craftsmanship.

· · · · · · · ·

In Virno's interpretation, this immaterialization of economic practice leads to a development that seems to be the opposite of what Sennett describes: rather than virtuosity disappearing due to the growing distance between labor and politics, the virtuosity of labor and that of politics begin to converge. As commodities, as well as the ways in which they are produced, become increasingly cultural, communicational, semiotic, expressive, and so on, the sphere of production takes on many of the characteristics that were traditionally assigned to the world of politics. Today, production, distribution, and consumption are predicated on a techno-cultural infrastructure enabling constant multidimensional flows of communication. This is to say that today's regime of production runs on a techno-cultural platform sustaining a publicly organized space that in a very strange manner resembles that of politics. The virtuosity required by such a space is one that is immediately and radically social. It implies the permanent presence of others as co-producers, co-distributors, co-consumers. So the new virtuosity is intrinsically relational, even performative. And yet, at the same time, it is nothing special - at least not in the sense of involving genius or special skill. As Virno puts it,

> virtuosity is nothing unusual, nor does it require some special talent. One need only think of the process whereby someone who speaks draws on the inexhaustible potential of language (the opposite of a defined "work") to create an utterance that is entirely of the moment and unrepeatable.[55]

· · · · · · · · ·

Today's regime of production runs on a techno-cultural platform
sustaining a publicly organized space that in a very strange manner
resembles that of politics.

· · · · · · · · ·

This kind of virtuosity marks a moment in the development of the human species in which our basic socio-linguistic faculties, i.e., the human ability to creatively communicate, have become productive. Robert Reich has, already more than twenty years ago, highlighted this fact when writing about the growing importance of so-called 'symbolic analysts' within the economy.[56] Since then, the spectrum of activity that applies virtuosity for the sake of generating economic value has expanded massively. From the growing sector of services with (at least) a smile to the quickly evolving business models based on social and mobile media, a kind of public space re-emerges, although one in which potentially emancipative proto-political practice is perpetually transformed into intensified labor.

What we are confronted with is thus a situation in which the old economic training ground for good citizens has become a site itself requiring political skills to begin with. This lack of what Sloterdijk would call Übungsraum is one of the reasons for our current political and cultural disorientation. If the generation of economic value today takes place in a proto-political arena of instant communicative presence and connection, the *citoyen* merges with the bourgeois into the 21st century figure of the new virtuoso. For the new virtuoso, the idea of politics and economy being clearly divided social spheres has become obsolete. Her or his breeding ground and habitat is a plane of political-economic topology, best described as a practical Mobius strip where one is always on both sides at the same time.

## Conclusion

The good news is that all over the global metropolis, one can observe experiments in building such topologies where the multitudinous powers of invention find their virtuous expressions. There are elements of such a topological reinvention of *bourgeois/citoyen* to be found in movements such as slow food, city farming, transition towns, guerrilla gardening, and indeed in the making of autonomous spaces while having to interact with existing legislation and funding schemes, as Urban Resort did with the Volkskrant building. From a new generation of squatters to digital bohemians, there is a network of topological laboratories specializing in bottom-up social restructuring. Of course, this development is still in its early stages and there is also always the possibility for the eroding institutions of industrial discipline and asceticism to be replaced by structures of a digital police state and/or neoliberal market-arrangements.

· · · · · · · ·

This lack of what Sloterdijk would call Übungsraum is
one of the reasons for our current political and
cultural disorientation.

· · · · · · · ·

What is at stake then, in experiments such as the Volkskrant building, is the evolution of Sennett's old craftsman shop into a topology of contemporary virtuosity. With reference to Sennett and Virno, it seems evident that a space like the Volkskrant building indeed took on many of the facets one would expect from a contemporary equivalent of the craftsman's workshop. The lessons of the Volkskrant building, that we tried to record in this book, are a valuable input in the important quest for *Übungsräume* that provide training grounds for the kind of virtuosity that is able to topologically transform precarity into networked strength. Instead of a para-political practice turned into intensified social labor for corporate exploitation, a more emancipative form of participation in society is rendered possible by way of performative defiance.

All this is still a far cry away from a perfect model of an infrastructure for 21st century virtuosity. Among other things, it begs the question of how such topologies of citizenship might be extended to those parts of the multitude that are clearly underrepresented in co-working spaces and art factories, such as migrants and those less well-versed in the ways of contemporary entrepreneurial virtuosity. The example of the Volkskrant building is far from providing the final answer to this question, but it has offered a trajectory of failing forward which may provide a basis for those courageous enough to take up the task themselves.

Canvas as it looked throughout 2012 and 2013.

# ENDNOTES

1 Jamie Peck, 'Recreative City: Amsterdam, Vehicular Ideas and the Adaptive Spaces of Creativity Policy', *Journal of Urban and Regional Research* 36:3 (2012): 462-485.

2 Charles Landry, *The Creative City: A Toolkit for Urban Innovators*, London: Earthscan, 2008. Ned Rossiter and Geert Lovink, MyCreativity Reader: *A Critique of Creative Industries*, Amsterdam: Institute of Network Cultures, 2007.

3 Richard Florida, *The Rise of The Creative Class: And How It's Transforming Work, Leisure, Community, and Everyday Life*, New York: Basic Books, 2002.

4 Roel Griffioen, 'Hoe de broedplaats een surrogaat voor echte stedelijke ontwikkeling werd', September 2014, https://decorrespondent.nl/1713/Hoe-de-broedplaats-een-excuus-voor-echte-stedelijke-ontwikkeling-werd/130465691004-fa40aeca.

5 Edward Soja, 'The Stimulus of a Little Confusion', in Léon Deben, Willem Heinemeijer, Dick van der Vaart (eds) *Understanding Amsterdam: Essays on Economic Vitality, City Life and Urban Form*, Amsterdam: Het Spinhuis. 2000.

6 Soja, 'The Stimulus of a Little Confusion', p. 119.

7 Soja, 'The Stimulus of a Little Confusion', p. 119.

8 Soja, 'The Stimulus of a Little Confusion', p. 119.

9 Eric Duivenvoorden, *Een voet tussen de deur: geschiedenis van de kraakbeweging* [1964-1999], Amsterdam: De Arbeiderspers, 2000. Eric Duivenvoorden, *Het Kroningsoproer: 30 april 1980, reconstructie van een historisch keerpunt*, Amsterdam: De Arbeiderspers, 2005.

10 Bilwet, *Bewegingsleer*, Amsterdam: Ravijn, 1990, p. 37, translation by the authors.

11 Bilwet, *Bewegingsleer*, p. 37.

12 For more information on Provo see the following books: Roel van Duyn, *Provo: De geschiedenis van de provotarische beweging 1965-1967*, Amsterdam: Meulenhoff, 1985; Eric Duivenvoorden, *Magiër van een nieuwe tijd: het leven van Jasper Grootveld*, Amsterdam: Arbeiderspers, 2009.

13 Bilwet, *Bewegingsleer*, p. 40, translation by the authors.

14 Nederpunk.punt.nl, 'Krakers en punks deel 2 (panden in Amsterdam)', 26 November 2005, http://nederpunk.punt.nl/content/2005/11/krakers-en-punks-deel-2-panden-in-amsterdam.

15 The 'dark side' of the squatters movement has been captured extensively in the documentary *De stad was van ons* (dir. Joost Seelen and Eric Duivenvoorden, 1996), downloadable at: https://www.youtube.com/watch?v=dfPKwFB6WpY.

16 Jaap Stam, 'Wij zijn een makelaar voor tegendraadse types', *De Volkskrant*,16 February 2013, http://www.volkskrant.nl/vk/nl/2844/Archief/archief/article/detail/3394765/2013/01/16/Wij-zijn-een-makelaar-voor-tegendraadse-types.dhtml.

17 Jaap Evert Abrahamse et al, *Spel + Tegenspel: supervisie aan de IJ-oevers*, Bussum: Toth, 2000.

18 'Geen cultuur zonder subcultuur', http://bongersite.nl/broedplaats401.html.

19 'Geen cultuur zonder subcultuur', translation by the authors.

20 Bart van Zoelen, 'Niet de zoveelste atelierbunker: Kraakveteranen huren en verhuren het Volkskrant-gebouw', *Het Parool*, 2 June 2007.

21 Fred Triep, 'Openingspeech meeting Urban Resort in old VK building', *YouTube*, 3 June 2007, http://www.youtube.com/watch?v=XV5yTkt-svQ.

22 Fred Triep, 'Presentation of the International Amsterdam Group 1', *YouTube*, 1 June 2007, http://www.youtube.com/watch?v=Wyv-n_J-YE8.

23 Sarah Gehrke, 'Very well bred: Newspaper building re-opens as an urban resort for the arts', Amsterdam Weekly, 27 September - 3 October 2007.

24 Saskia Sassen, *The Global City: New York, London, Tokyo*, Princeton: Princeton University Press, 2013.

25 Manfred Ertel, 'Amsterdam', *Der Spiegel*, 20 August 2007.

26 Ertel, 'Amsterdam'.

27 Liedewij Loorbach, 'Gaan!', *Het Parool*, 22 March 2008.

28 Judith Laanen, 'La Melodia: "Bam! En iedereen is om"', *LiveXS*, March 2008.

29 Douglas Heingartner, 'Beast in Show', *Time Out Amsterdam*, October 2008.

30 'Kunstspeeltjes van dode hond en kat', *Het Parool*, 24 October 2008.

31 Liedewij Loorbach, 'Muziek maken met koffieschotels', *Het Parool*, 7 May 2009.

32 Bureaubroedplaatsen, 'Volkskrant Gebouw aflevering 2: Beveiligen', *YouTube*, 19 April 2012, http://www.youtube.com/watch?v=UYkR0EdZK3k.

33 Bas van de Geyn and Jaap Draaisma, 'The Embrace of Amsterdam's Creative Breeding Ground', in Libby Porter and Kate Shaw (eds) *Whose Urban Renaissance? An International Comparison of Urban Regeneration Strategies*, London: Routledge, 2009.

34 Plek in de Stad, 'Aynouk Tan - Spuistraat', AT5, 8 juli 2014, http://www.at5.nl/tv/plek-in-de-stad/aflevering/15777.

35 Bregje Lampe, 'Feesten volgens Visjuweel', *Het Parool*, 9 December 2008.

36 Jaus Müller, 'Een hoop no-nonsense en lelijkheid bij Canvas', *nrc.next*, 18 September 2008.

37 Joel Weickgenant, 'A Different Kind of Spin, After the News Has Gone', *The New York Times*, 1 April 2009.

38 Steven Verseput, 'Broedplaatsen voor zakelijke vrijdenkers', *NRC Handelsblad*, 6 March 2013.

39 Sebastian Olma, 'Die Topologisierung der Wertschoepfung', in Bastian Lange and Malte Bergmann (eds) *Eigensinnige Geographien*, Wiesbaden: VS Verlag, 2011. Sebastian Olma and Tonia Welter, *Das Beta-Prinzip: Coworking und die Zukunft der Arbeit*, Berlin: Blumbar, 2011.

40 Pascal Gielen, *Creativity and other Fundamentalisms*, Amsterdam: Mondriaan Fonds, 2013.

41 David Hesmondhalgh and Sarah Baker, *Creative Labour: Media Work in Three Cultural Industries*, New York: Routledge, 2011.

42 Maurizio Lazzarato, *Les Révolutions du Capitalisme*, Paris: Les Empêcheurs de Penser en Rond/ Le Seuil, 2004.

43 Sebastian Olma, *'Autonomy by Dissent'*, in EHBK/OT301, Autonomy by Dissent, Amsterdam: EHBK/OT301, 2013.

44 This was illustrated by the Global Uprisings conference, held from 15 until 17 November 2013, in which global protest movements were connected to local spaces for autonomous practice through lectures and events.

45 See, for instance, the extensive public program at Pakhuis de Zwijger.

46 Emile Durkheim, *The Elementary Forms of the Religious Life*, London: George Allen & Unwin, 1915.

47 Max Weber, *Economy and Society: An Outline of Interpretative Sociology*, New York: Bedminster Press, 1968.

48 Norbert Elias, *The Civilizing Process: Sociogenetic and Psychogenetic Investigations*, Oxford: Blackwell Publishers, 2000.

49 Michel Foucault, *Discipline & Punish: The Birth of the Prison*, New York: Random House, 1995.

50 Peter Sloterdijk, *Du musst dein Leben ändern: Über Anthropotechnik*, Frankfurt am Main: Suhrkamp Verlag. 2009.

51 Sloterdijk, *Du musst dein Leben ändern*, p. 497.

52 'The argument […] is that the craft of making physical things provides insights into the techniques of experience that can shape our dealings with others. Both the difficulties and the possibilities of making things well apply to making human relationships. Material challenges like working with resistance or managing ambiguity are instructive in understanding the resistance people harbour to one another or the uncertain boundaries between people. I've stressed the positive open role routine and practicing play in the work of crafting physical things; so too do people need to practice their relations with one another, learn the skills of anticipation and revision in order to improve these relations. […] [W]ho we are arises directly from what our bodies can do. Social consequences are built into the structure and the functioning of the human body, as in the workings of the human hand. I argue no more and no less than that the capacities our bodies have to shape physical things are the same capacities we draw on in social contacts'. In: Richard Sennett, *The Craftsman*, Yale: Yale University Press, 2008, pp. 289-290.

53 The following by now classical works address this question. Luc Boltanski and Eve Chiapello, *Le nouvel esprit du capitalisme*, Paris: Gallimard, 1999 and Holm Friebe and Sascha Lobo, *Die digitale Boheme oder: Intelligentes Leben jenseits der Festanstellung*, München: Random House, 2006.

54 Paolo Virno, *A Grammar of the Multitude: For an Analysis of Contemporary Forms of Life*, Los Angeles/New York: Semiotext(e), 2004.

55 Virno, *A Grammar of the Multitude*, p. 195.

56 Robert Reich, *The Work of Nations*, New York: Vintage Books, 1992.

## REFERENCE LIST

Abrahamse, Jaap Evert et al. Spel + *Tegenspel: supervisie aan de IJ-oevers*, Bussum: Toth, 2000.

Bilwet. *Bewegingsleer*, Amsterdam: Ravijn, 1990.

Boltanski, Luc and Eve Chiapello. *Le nouvel esprit du capitalisme*, Paris: Gallimard, 1999.

*De stad was van ons* (dir. Joost Seelen and Eric Duivenvoorden, 1996), downloadable at https://www.youtube.com/watch?v=dfPKwFB6WpY.

Duivenvoorden, Eric. *Een Voet Tussen De Deur: geschiedenis van de kraakbeweging* [1964-1999], Amsterdam: De Arbeiderspers, 2000.

Duivenvoorden, Eric. *Het Kroningsoproer: 30 april 1980, reconstructie van een historisch keerpunt*, Amsterdam: De Arbeiderspers, 2005.

Duivenvoorden, Eric. *Magiër van een nieuwe tijd: het leven van Robert Jasper Grootveld*, Amsterdam: Arbeiderspers, 2009.

Durkheim, Emile. *The Elementary Forms of the Religious Life*, London: George Allen & Unwin, 1915.

Duyn, Roel van. *Provo: De geschiedenis van de provotarische beweging 1965-1967*, Amsterdam: Meulenhoff, 1985.

Elias, Norbert. *The Civilizing Process: Sociogenetic and Psychogenetic Investigations*, Oxford: Blackwell Publishers, 2000.

Ertel, Manfred. 'Amsterdam', *Der Spiegel*, 20 August 2007.

Florida, Richard. *The Rise of The Creative Class: And How It's Transforming Work, Leisure, Community, and Everyday Life*, New York: Basic Books, 2002.

Foucault, Michel. *Discipline & Punish: the Birth of the Prison*, New York: Random *House*, 1995.

Friebe, Holm and Sascha Lobo. *Die digitale Boheme oder: Intelligentes Leben jenseits der Festanstellung*, München: Random House, 2006.

'Geen cultuur zonder subcultuur', http://bongersite.nl/broedplaats401.html.

Gehrke, Sarah. 'Very well bred: Newspaper building re-opens as an urban resort for the arts', Amsterdam Weekly, 27 September - 3 October 2007.

Geyn, Bas van de and Jaap Draaisma. 'The Embrace of Amsterdam's Creative Breeding Ground', in Libby Porter and Kate Shaw (eds) *Whose Urban Renaissance? An International Comparison of Urban Regeneration Strategies*, London: Routledge, 2009.

Gielen, Pascal. *Creativity and other Fundamentalisms*, Amsterdam: Mondriaan Fonds, 2013.

Griffioen, Roel. 'Hoe de broedplaats een surrogaat voor echte stedelijke ontwikkeling werd', September 2014, https://decorrespondent.nl/1713/Hoe-de-broedplaats-een-excuus-voor-echte-stedelijke-ontwikkeling-werd/130465691004-fa40aeca.

Heingartner, Douglas. 'Beast in Show', *Time Out Amsterdam*, 1-31 October 2008.

Hesmondhalgh, David and Sarah Baker. *Creative Labour: Media Work in Three Cultural Industries*, New York: Routledge, 2011.

Nederpunk.punt.nl. 'Krakers en punks deel 2 (panden in Amsterdam)', 26 November 2005, http://nederpunk.punt.nl/content/2005/11/krakers-en-punks-deel-2-panden-in-amsterdam.

'Kunstspeeltjes van dode hond en kat', *Het Parool*, 24 October 2008.

Laanen, Judith. 'La Melodia: "Bam! En iedereen is om"', *LiveXS*, March 2008.

Lampe, Bregje. 'Feesten volgens Visjuweel', *Het Parool*, 9 December 2008.

Landry, Charles. *The Creative City: A Toolkit for Urban Innovators*, London: Earthscan, 2008.

Lazzarato, Maurizio. *Les Révolutions du Capitalisme*, Paris: Les Empêcheurs de Penser en Rond/ Le Seuil, 2004.

Loorbach, Liedewij. 'Gaan!', *Het Parool*, 22 March 2008.

Loorbach, Liedewij. 'Muziek maken met koffieschotels', *Het Parool*, 7 May 2009.

Müller, Jaus. 'Een hoop no-nonsense en lelijkheid bij Canvas', *nrc.next*, 18 September 2008.

Olma, Sebastian. 'Autonomy by Dissent' in EHBK/OT301, *Autonomy by Dissent*, Amsterdam: EHBK/OT301, 2013.

Olma, Sebastian. 'Die Topologisierung der Wertschoepfung', in Bastian Lange and Malte Bergmann (eds) *Eigensinnige Geographien*, Wiesbaden: VS Verlag, 2011.

Olma, Sebastian and Tonia Welter. *Das Beta-Prinzip: Coworking und die Zukunft der Arbeit*, Berlin: Blumbar, 2011.

Fred Triep, 'Openingspeech meeting Urban Resort in old VK building', *YouTube*, 3 June 2007, https://www.youtube.com/watch?v=XV5yTkt-svQ.

Plek in de Stad, 'Aynouk Tan - Spuistraat', AT5, 8 juli 2014, http://www.at5.nl/tv/plek-in-de-stad/aflevering/15777.

Fred Triep, 'Presentation of the International Amsterdam Group 1', *YouTube*, 1 June 2007, http://www.youtube.com/watch?v=Wyv-n_J-YE8.

Reich, Robert. *The Work of Nations*, New York: Vintage Books, 1992.

Rossiter, Ned and Geert Lovink. *MyCreativity Reader: A Critique of Creative Industries*, Amsterdam: Institute of Network Cultures, 2007.

Sassen, Saskia. *The Global City: New York, London, Tokyo*, Princeton: Princeton University Press, 2013.

Sennett, Richard. *The Craftsman*, Yale: Yale University Press, 2008.

Sloterdijk, Peter. *Du musst dein Leben ändern: Über Anthropotechnik*, Frankfurt am Main: Suhrkamp Verlag, 2009.

Soja, Edward. 'The Stimulus of a Little Confusion', in Léon Deben, Willem Heinemeijer, Dick van der Vaart (eds) *Understanding Amsterdam: Essays on Economic Vitality, City Life and Urban Form*, Amsterdam: Het Spinhuis, 2000.

Stam, Jaap. 'Wij zijn een makelaar voor tegendraadse types', *De Volkskrant*, 16 February 2013, http://www.volkskrant.nl/vk/nl/2844/Archief/archief/article/detail/3394765/2013/01/16/Wij-zijn-een-makelaar-voor-tegendraadse-types.dhtml.

Verseput, Steven. 'Broedplaatsen voor zakelijke vrijdenkers', *NRC Handelsblad*, 6 March 2013.

Virno, Paolo. *A Grammar of the Multitude: For an analysis of contemporary forms of life*, Los Angeles/New York: Semiotext(e), 2004.

'Volkskrantgebouw aflevering 2: Beveiligen', https://www.youtube.com watch?v=UYkROEdZK3k. Weber, Max. *Economy and Society: An Outline of Interpretative Sociology*, New York: Bedminster Press, 1968.

Weickgenant, Joel. 'A Different Kind of Spin, After the News Has Gone', *The New York Times*, 1 April 2009.

Zoelen, Bart van. 'Niet de zoveelste atelierbunker: Kraakveteranen huren en verhuren het Volkskrant-gebouw', *Het Parool*, 2 June 2007.